"Jennifer Freed is one of my f... fresh wisdom in *A Map to Your Soul* is a North Star.

Glennon Doyle, author of the #1 *New York Times* bestseller *Untamed*, founder of Together Rising

"While journeying through the pages of *A Map to Your Soul*, it is wholly evident that Jennifer Freed truly cares about the lives of her readers. She wants your life to feel good and be meaningful. Whether you are interested in astrology or not, this book is filled with wise and practical offerings that I have no doubt will either help you find the path you've been looking for, or continue on your current path more confidently."

—Cleo Wade, *New York Times* bestselling author of *Heart Talk*

"Dr. Jen is an incredibly intuitive guide who helps folks recognize their strengths and potential. She provides a clear map to realizing your innate gifts and how to best share them with the world."

—Mila Kunis

"Dr. Jennifer Freed is a true voice and vision for a fully expressed life of love, creativity, and the celebration of our differences with dignity."

—Van Jones, author of *Beyond the Messy Truth*

"Dr. Jen speaks to the soul. She is a trustworthy guide on the most important subjects in our lives. Her book is a must-read!"

—Emily Morse, PhD, host of *Sex With Emily*

"Jennifer's work is thoughtful, illuminating, and powerful. She is a true master in her field."

—Stephanie Allynne & Tig Notaro

Jennifer Freed has thirty-eight years of experience working as a psychological astrologer and a PhD in psychology. In this practical guide to life, she shows you how to decode and tap into your unique strengths and quirks. Self-assessments and quizzes in every chapter help you determine your elemental balance, personalize your rituals and routines, and pinpoint your most effective strategies across different areas of your life. You'll learn about your ideal communication style, developing your intuition, honing creativity, building healthy habits, the home aesthetics that suit you best, what your core values say about you, and how to find more pleasure in your intimate relationships.

A Map to Your Soul is written with the beginner in mind but offers deep insight to the experienced student of astrology (and to anyone who wants to read the book guided by their astrological birth chart). This is a journey through the way the elements express themselves in your life. By balancing and supporting the elements within us, we can live a more vibrant life—and fulfill our soul's purpose.

A MAP TO YOUR SOUL

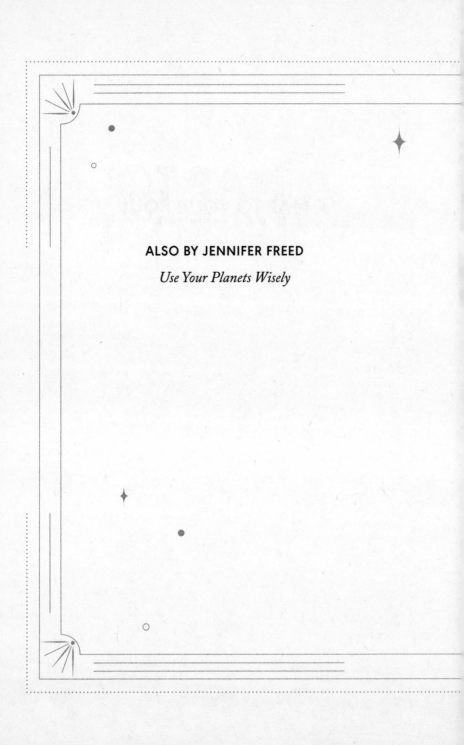

ALSO BY JENNIFER FREED

Use Your Planets Wisely

A MAP TO YOUR SOUL

Using the Astrology of Fire, Earth, Air, and Water to Live Deeply and Fully

Jennifer Freed, PhD

goop
PRESS

RODALE.
NEW YORK

RODALE and the Plant colophon are registered trademarks of
Penguin Random House LLC.

Library of Congress Cataloging-in-Publication Data
Names: Freed, Jennifer, 1958– author.
Title: A map to your soul / Jennifer Freed Ph.D.
Description: New York : Goop Press/Rodale, [2022] | Includes index.
Identifiers: LCCN 2022013389 (print) | LCCN 2022013390 (ebook) |
ISBN 9780593236154 (hardcover) | ISBN 9780593236161 (ebook)
Subjects: LCSH: Houses (Astrology) | Self-actualization (Psychology)
Classification: LCC BF1716 .F74 2022 (print) | LCC BF1716 (ebook) |
DDC 133.5/3042—dc23/eng/20220505

ISBN 978-0-593-23615-4
Ebook ISBN 978-0-593-23616-1

Printed in the United States of America

Book design and earth icon illustration by Andrea Lau
Cover design and illustration by Vi-An Nguyen
Fire, air, and water icon illustrations by Shutterstock.com/fivestar_studio

10 9 8 7 6 5 4 3 2 1

First Edition

Dedicated to Rendy,
whose love has made all the elements sing

CONTENTS

ACKNOWLEDGMENTS

I want my acknowledgments expressed before you even read this book—because frankly, without these people, this book would never have happened.

To the glamorous goof (GP), who had the courage, the caring, the vision, and the perseverance to make a world of possibilities for women who want to have fully expressed lives.

To Elise Loehnen, who discovered me and gave me the platform to share my gifts, and who continues to be a constant light in my cosmos.

To Melissa Lowenstein, who helped me write this book, and who shows up for life with more integrity, devotion, and talent than seems humanly possible.

To Coleen O'Shea, who is a badass agent, one of the smartest women I know, and an enormous anchor of compassion.

To Donna Loffredo, my editor, who truly makes everything shine. Donna, you have thrilled me with your wisdom and true grit.

To Kiki Koroshetz, who could run the world with heart, chutzpah, and soul. I wish she would.

To Leah Pellegrini, an outstanding writer and astrologer who contributed to the introductory explanation of astrology in Appendix 1: thank you.

To Monisha Holmes, a beautiful and radical astrologer who helped with the write-up about astrological house systems in Appendix 3: thank you.

Thank you, Jenny Blaise Kramer, for your input on the earliest iterations of this book.

To my sacred crew: you all had a major hand in supporting me. I thank you forever.

A MAP TO YOUR SOUL

INTRODUCTION

To forget how to dig the earth and
to tend the soil is to forget ourselves.

—MAHATMA GANDHI

No water, no life. No blue, no green.

—SYLVIA EARLE

Set your life on fire. Seek those who fan your flames.

—RUMI

That's life: starting over, one breath at a time.

—SHARON SALZBERG

This book is meant to help you live a fully expressed life.

What do I mean, exactly, by a fully expressed life? What does a fully expressed life look like? How would it feel? And why would you want one?

I'm talking about being, day to day, most of the time, in touch with yourself and the world that surrounds you. About being able to relate to pretty much anyone and everything in a healthy way. About living each day secure in the knowledge that you are developing your core gifts with discipline, devotion, and confidence, and about being able to enjoy your unique contributions in all arenas of your life, big and small.

It may be hard to imagine right now what it would be like to live a life each day expressing all facets of yourself. The explorations in this book will reveal what this kind of life looks like for you. It's exquisitely different for every person. We are so unique, and our gifts so complex, that no one-size-fits-all approach or singular road map can lead us to our own fully expressed life. This book is neither of those things (one-size-fits-all or singular road map); it is a guide for self-knowledge, self-revelation, wisdom in relationships, and finding your place of contribution in the universe, based on your distinctive strengths and preferences.

A fully expressed life is available to anyone who is willing to put in the work required to bring their natural gifts—and we all come in with many gifts—to fruition. *Agency* is required: this is the ability to actively put in time, to learn, to work toward something, to remain curious, to be willing to step out of our comfort zones and into the unknown, to fail fast and recover and reenter the arena of learning and growth. When we add in the imperative to do all that work not only for our own personal benefit, or even for the benefit of our close loved ones, but for the whole wide world, we aren't talking about just plain agency: we have entered the realm of *spiritual* agency.

This is not a book for anyone who is hoping for someone else to hand down easy answers to life's profound challenges. If that's what you're after, you'll have no trouble finding other books or approaches that teach you to be dependent on formulas, or a guru who would be more than happy to tell you who you are and who you should be. This book is for people who know that they hold their own answers within, and that they can only find their gold using their own specific treasure map. What they need is not to have answers given to them, but some prompting and guidance to find those answers for themselves. Here, psychological astrology is the source of that prompting and guidance.

What Is Psychological Astrology?

Astrology is often misused to prescribe solutions, attribute stereotypes, and make excuses for human behavior. Psychological astrology does none of these things. It is an evocative and inspiring inquiry into all your divine possibilities that honors the choice and responsibility you have over your life. It reveals you to yourself with a depth and breadth that empower you to navigate your life in the most satisfying and gratifying way possible. Modern astrology tends to focus on self-awareness: *Who are you, anyway? What's your true personality? What are you meant to do in this life?* My take on psychological astrology certainly will help you to know yourself better, but it will also support you in using that expanded self-knowledge and self-awareness to make your optimal contribution to your community and to your loved ones.

I have spent my entire adult life studying and practicing both psychology and astrology: human motivation, patterns, cultural indoctrination, and psychological complexes and methods as a psychologist, and the movements and meanings of the planets and the metaphors of the astrological signs as an astrologer. Psychological astrology is the study of the soul combined with the study of the stars—your biological and nurturing histories coupled with your cosmic DNA.

In my psychology training, I learned to understand and treat dysfunctional thinking, feeling, and behavior, and spent two decades learning and practicing methods for reducing the impact of generational and situational trauma. Within the educational universe of astrology, I learned to see and interpret the vastly complex lexicon of the planets and the stars and the ways in which their alignments reveal destinies and cycles. My practice of psychological astrology lies at the confluence of these two arts.

Beyond all of this training, reading thousands of client charts has taught me the most about the divine plan for each person's life. The readings I give are not downloads of information I extract from looking at people's charts while they listen intently; they are therapeutic conversations. I bring to them my expertise and knowledge of psychology and astrology, and they bring to me their deep and true knowledge of themselves. Together, we find our way to insights that often feel both new and familiar, that affirm things they already know, at some level, deep within themselves, and that inspire them to lean into their growing edges.

I owe my greatest astrological knowledge to my clients. Listening deeply to their stories of how the planets in their charts have corresponded to their life experiences is the foundation of my wisdom.

This book draws on both my intense training and my experiences with astrology and psychology. This is your soul map and your star map combined in one.

The Elements: An Introduction

The wisdom gleaned from the natural elements—fire, earth, air, and water—is a foundation of healing practices in Chinese, Native American, Vedic, and Tibetan cultures. This book will focus on the use of the elements in astrology.

You might be familiar with the elements as they correspond to your Sun sign—for example, Aries is fire, Taurus is earth, Gemini is air, and Cancer is water. But as you probably know, there is much more to your birth chart than your Sun sign, and similarly there is much more to your elemental makeup than the element that corresponds to your Sun sign.

Each of us has a unique constellation of the four elements inside of us that manifests in distinct ways in different areas of our lives. You may be fiery when challenged at work but grounded in earthy routine when it comes to your health. Or you might be an airy intellectual when it comes to love and a sensitive, watery empath when it comes to sex.

The four core elements of your soul are

fire, the dynamic, exuberant, action-oriented part of your nature earth, the grounded, sensual, conserving part of your nature

 air, the intellectual, objective, logical part of your nature

 water, the feeling, empathetic, merging, and sensitive part of your nature

Thousands of years ago, our ancestors lived in close contact with the earth and the hearth and relied on their ability to make fire. Their lives depended on fresh air and clean sources of water. We have just as much reliance on these four elements today, and they offer up indispensable wisdom for both survival and thriving.

We are *made* of fire, earth, air, and water. Electrical impulses zap throughout our bodies to stimulate our muscle cells and fire our neurons. Our carbon-based bodies are built from the very same building blocks as stones and soil. We can only go three minutes without air, and our body weight is 60 percent water. It's no exaggeration to say that we *are* the wisdom of the elements as we walk around, talking, hugging, making love, building skyscrapers, starting nonprofits, giving birth, lying on our deathbeds. We are the wisdom of the elements thinking, feeling, loving, experiencing, learning, questioning, and exploring.

As we tend to the four elements, we start to balance ourselves with nature. And when we become more aware of the elements in our daily lives, we build the resources and energies to contribute to our friends, family, and community.

Think of a time when you felt the most grounded and centered (earth), the most mentally clear (air), the most openhearted (water), and the most creative (fire). That was most likely a time in your life where you were most generous, open, and willing to contribute to the well-being of other people. See if you can revisit that space in your mind for long enough to feel it in your body.

In our culture, we've forgotten to recognize our elemental connection to everything around us. Some might argue that this is a main reason why we now face intense and escalating climate change, which brings drought, floods, forest fires, and deadly storms, as well as widespread contamination

> ✦
>
> Everything in the universe is within you. Ask all from yourself.
>
> –Rumi (he had Moon in Libra opposed by Neptune)

of earth, air, and water. We deny our deep connection to the natural world at our own peril. It is time to bring elemental wisdom back into everyday awareness, in a way that honors how much things have changed since humankind first made fire.

When you start your mindful practice of noticing each element, and take the time to truly appreciate its simplicity and power, you begin to shape your brain in ways that return it to its most natural, most resilient state. Remember, when you take just one gulp of clean, fresh mountain air, in that moment, that's enough. When you stand in a gorgeous field looking at magnificent redwood trees, seeing that bounty of earth is enough.

When you are near a beautiful fire, whether it's outdoors camp-
ing or indoors keeping you cozy, staring at the magic of that fire
is enough. And when you are enjoying an exquisite bath or
shower or dipping in the ocean or a pool and feeling cleansed
and renewed and open, that is enough.

The Domains

This book is a twelve-part journey into making your most exciting possibilities a reality, guided by the elements of fire, earth, air,
and water. It will unlock your completely individual elemental
codes, with each chapter delving into the interplay of elements
within a specific *domain* of life.

The domains are based on the astrological house system,
which divides the experience of being alive in a human body
into twelve areas. This system for organizing our life experiences
into parts is, to my knowledge, the very best one that exists not
only for the development of the self but also for the development of relationships with other individuals and with the collective of all other people. Finally, it develops the self as a microcosm
of the universe. Each human being contains within them the
ingredients of all of life—all four elements—and the elements
are expressed uniquely across each person's twelve domains. Exploring this system for yourself will support you in best expressing those qualities that are uniquely yours, and that also
contribute to the web of all human life.

I have chosen to refer to "domains" rather than the astrological houses themselves for two reasons: first, because each

house refers to many areas of life, and I want to focus on just one or two of those areas—the parts I've found to be most valuable to consider on the path to full expression; and second, because I want this book to work for everyone, whether they have astrological knowledge or not.

Understanding and being able to navigate the house system in astrology is not a requirement for folks who want to take this ride with me, but knowing more about the houses in astrology will only bolster your understanding of the domains as I'll describe them. (If you are interested in expanding your knowledge of the houses, you can refer to Appendix 2.)

As you work your way through this book, these domains will become your framework for examining the dance of the elements in your life.

> We need Joy as we need air. We need Love as we need water. We need each other as we need the earth we share.
>
> —Maya Angelou (she had the Moon in the air sign Libra, opposed by radical and inventive Uranus)

Looking Ahead

As you go through these twelve chapters, you will have abundant opportunities to assess yourself and to enhance your understanding of the people in your life. As you develop your own magical formulas for synthesizing the elements, you will come to feel like life is going *with* you instead of against you. You will develop confidence in your skills to regain your equilibrium when you realize you are out of balance.

THE DOMAINS

The twelve domains are based on the twelve astrological houses. Each domain represents a different area of life:

First house: awareness of self, appearance, outward personality

Second house: values and personal resources like money and skills

Third house: thought and communication

Fourth house: home, parenting, inner security

Fifth house: creativity, romance, fun, children

Sixth house: work, health, self-improvement, self-care, daily service

Seventh house: partnership, including marriage

Eighth house: sex, death, other people's money, sharing, surrender

Ninth house: philosophy, higher education, publishing, religion, long trips

Tenth house: career, status, reputation

Eleventh house: groups, friends, community contribution

Twelfth house: spirituality, solitude, institutions, transcendence

As this house system provides a perfect map for examining our attainments and possibilities, I've used it as a frame for the twelve domains in this book.

How to Use This Book

You don't need any previous astrological knowledge to benefit from *The Elements*. It is a book for all people who want to have a more fulfilled life. The assessments and practices in this book will reveal the same truths about you and your elemental strengths, weaknesses, and areas ripe for growth whether you relate them to your astrological chart or not.

Put another way, let's say you choose to engage wholeheartedly in the processes laid out in this book before even looking at your natal chart. You could then obtain a chart and a report, or even a reading with a psychological astrologer, and I'm willing to bet that you would find everything you learned here affirmed. You would already have done the work of knowing yourself deeply through the chapters covering each domain.

That being said, those with some knowledge of astrology (or those who would like to add that dimension to their knowledge) get a few extras in this book. You'll find special ""*Illuminations" tips designed for you. If you have a basic understanding of the birth chart—which would include knowing the signs, understanding the houses, and knowing how to read the elements within each house—you may want to refer to your chart as you move through the exercises. Going through these inventories and assessments with your chart as a reference can expand the learning and growth possible with this material. You'll be able to see the balance of elements in your chart and how they correlate to the answers you give for each of the assessments.

Each of the astrological houses in your birth chart is "ruled" by one of the twelve astrological signs. And the astrological signs have elemental makeups: Aries, Leo, and Sagittarius are fire; Taurus, Virgo, and Capricorn are earth; Gemini, Libra, and Aquarius are air; and Cancer, Scorpio, and Pisces are water. You'll see them mentioned from time to time, as the element related to each house/domain in your chart will influence your natural gifts and growing edges in each area.

If you are completely new to astrology or want a less intense learning experience, you can simply enjoy the assessment tools and the practical exercises for your own betterment and happiness; or you can turn to Appendix 1 for a general introduction to astrology.

✦

ILLUMINATIONS

A note for advanced seekers: If you are already familiar with the language of astrology, or if you simply have high motivation to squeeze every last bit of wisdom you can from this book, you may want to obtain a copy of your natal chart and a report that explains the chart fairly extensively. Many websites now offer free chart generation and reports; Cafe Astrology and Astro.com are two that I would recommend. All you need to do is enter your birth date, time, and place, and voilà!—you'll have a free chart and report in hand.

Please keep in mind, however, that a computer can never account for the total complexity of your unique experience and inner knowing. No algorithm can capture you in your true essence. A computerized report from a free online source is just a beginning. My recommendation to any advanced seeker is to get a legitimate reading from a skilled psychological astrologer in order to fully grasp the dance of the heavens in your chart, and your own best ways to explore your patterns and opportunities. Visit www.jenniferfreed.com for recommendations for fabulous psychological astrologers.

In each of these twelve chapters, you'll learn how to use the elements to your benefit and to the benefit of others within a specific domain of life experience. Each chapter contains an assessment tool—quizzes or self-evaluations where you'll be invited to reflect and self-examine. These inventories will support your personal investigation of all the things that truly matter for a fully lived and expressed life. One important note: *Even if you know your chart, take each quiz or assessment without layering your knowledge of astrology onto it.* Only after you have fully digested your results from the inventories should you consider how your astrological chart corresponds to your answers. The inventories will draw out more surprising insights for you if you approach them that way. Even astrological experts stand to learn more about themselves—and about astrology—by tackling these inventories from a beginner's mindset.

Each set of inventories is accompanied by practices that you can do on your own or with others to heighten or improve the expression of all four elements in that area of your life. Each chapter also includes true stories of personal growth related to the domain being addressed.

You can move through the book in a number of ways:

The one-year course. You may choose to complete each chapter over a month of deeply engaged inquiry and action. If you are more thoughtful and measured in your approach to learning and growth, you will probably get the most from savoring each chapter over a month or so, absorbing and metabolizing every nugget you can for as long as your soul wants.

Taking the book as a twelve-week course. If you're speedy and grabby, like me, you may want to plunge in and whiz through a chapter a week for twelve weeks. If this is how you end up moving through this book, don't be surprised if you feel a little exhausted at the finish and need to take a break for a while before you come back to it.

Selecting pieces that speak the most strongly to you right now. Each of these chapters is a self-contained unit. There's no imperative to go in order; you can pick and choose which chapters to focus on based on your current need or preference.

Sharing with friends, family, or colleagues. Looking at this book with someone you care about will enhance your appreciation of each other's unique makeups and help you learn how to encourage one another's deepest gifts. You can ask friends or family to go through this book with you as an activity to build self-awareness, empathy, and closeness. You can bring it to your work environment, focusing on chapters that feel appropriate to that setting to promote collegiality, productivity, and that elusive sense of truly knowing the people you work with every day.

Exploring with a partner or spouse. Having been a therapist for forty years, I can tell you that exploring these chapters as a couple will be transformative for your partnership.

Elemental Strengths

Within this book, you will find secret passageways to recognizing and utilizing your strengths. You'll discover strengths that you may never have considered before, as well as strengths that feel familiar and can be built upon with recognition, affirmation, and conscious application and practice.

For example, in my astrology chart, my strengths are fire and air. So no matter what's happening in my life, I can lean into my ability to think and speak clearly—air—and my incredible gut instincts, optimism, and dynamism—fire—to accomplish even the most tedious of earthly deeds, like paying bills or taxes. With whatever I tackle, I come from a place of fiery play and mental clarity fueled by a visionary overview.

Where I feel less strong is in the areas of earth and water: groundedness and deliberation are sometimes truly challenging for me. To balance my natural strengths, I need to maintain conscious practices to enhance earth and water in my life: a grounding, mindful daily qigong practice (earth), a practice of consciously slowing down around my tendency to blurt and run people over with my boundless enthusiasm (earth), and a practice of empathy and space holding for people I care about who are having all the big feelings and need a listening ear (water).

My partner is nearly all water.

Inside human beings/is where God learns.

—*Rainer Maria Rilke*

(he had the Sun and Mercury in Sagittarius and the Moon and Mars in Aquarius)

Water is about feeling; about kindness, tenderness, softness, holding, and sensitivity. She can approach even the most challenging discussions and the most annoying people with grace and compassion. Just like water, she wraps her softness around a situation. Everyone behaves better when she's around because they feel bathed in her luminous, generous, flowing warmth. Her areas of growth are fire, earth, and air. Like me, she has intentionally worked to strengthen her expression of the elements that aren't naturally strong for her. What's true, though, is that her watery depth and compassion is her superpower, just as my fire and air are my superpowers.

Playing Your Part

The times that we're in are extremely chaotic. We're seeing all kinds of protests and challenges to existing social structures and traditions alongside fabulous innovations and discoveries about the best way into an equitable and sustainable future. We are caught in an enduring, ever-worsening climate crisis and persistent economic and social disparities. This book is a pathway to your becoming an engaged and fully expressed global participant who can contribute to solutions. Doing your part could be the tipping point in making the whole world a safer, more sustainable, and hospitable place for all beings. Finding your way to your most fully expressed life frees you up to do your part.

We have built such status around being extraordinary and famous that it's hard for individual people to see how much they matter. Every single person has the capacity to help, inspire, and take a stand for a better world for all. Some will reach a wide audience; so be it. Some will have their impact just within their family, or with a few key friends, or with animals. All these are legacy enough. We can all take a seat at the table where heroes sit.

Every single person, **including you.**

This is the ultimate purpose of the exploration you will undertake through this book: yes, there will be self-knowledge and self-improvement, and an improvement in the way you feel day to day; but I want to encourage you not to stop there.

There is no small or insignificant part to play in the game of life. You are the only person who gets to play your part. We all need to support each other to land on what really deserves to be recognized and celebrated in our fellow humans and ourselves: not the number of social media likes or followers or any other indicator of the amount of public attention someone receives, but the unique, powerful, sacred effort and essence of each human being.

I'm sure we can all agree that true feelings of worth come from loving fully, being loved well, and having just enough support and security and safety to live a life that has true virtue and meaning. It is imperative, in this time, that we recognize our responsibility to provide this not just for ourselves but also for each other; and that this can happen in small ways every single day, in our everyday interactions.

Begin by going through this book with humility and dedication. As you learn and grow, also begin to see the beautiful expressions of the elements in unsung heroes in your life that do even their small part perfectly. Notice the warmth of the grocer. Notice the helpfulness of the server at a restaurant. Notice the joy of the delivery person. Notice the kind air of the folks who get paid to answer phones. They all want—as my friend Jen Buffett says—to be "safe, seen, and celebrated."

What does it mean to live in an animated, enchanted universe in which we are connected to the signals, signs, and metaphors of nature itself? It means that instead of seeing ourselves and our small egos as in charge of what happens and trying to manifest from a place of self-interest, we see ourselves as part of a symphony of manifestation, supported by an intelligent and sentient universe. It means that we are not intended to be cogs in a wheel, but specks of stardust packed with possibility.

Most of us are disconnected from nature, caught up in the digital demands of the modern world, hurtling headlong through fast-paced, busy lives. The antidote to the emptiness, anxiety, and sadness this disconnection can bring is found by balancing the elements. In this balance, we can truly flourish.

CHAPTER ONE

The First Domain:
The First Impression

Think about the first time you met a significant person in your life. They could be significant because you like or love them, or because they harmed or hurt you in some way.

See if you can take yourself back to the moment you met them or first saw them. How did you see them? How did they feel to you? What did you pick up on in that first encounter? And once you got to know them, how much did your first impression capture that person's most essential qualities?

The question of who we are when we first meet someone—how we appear to them when we've just walked into the room, before we even say hello—is the focus of the first domain of experience: the *persona* or the *mask*.

Every person wears a mask; every person has a persona that comes forward as a first impression. Each of us has a front that we show to the world. This is not at all disingenuous or fake; it's neither bad nor good. The mask is just a way that we filter the world and the world filters us in those first encounters. It is a social strategy that is developed by all human beings at quite an early age, and it is a true source of our strengths and gifts.

Your Assigned Role

In our family of origin, we are each assigned certain roles. Some of us are assigned to be the funny one. Others are designated to be highly responsible; others, to be the superstar performers; others, to be the truth-tellers, willing to name the unnameable; and still others to be seen and not heard. Every one of us can recall the assignment we received in our early years, and we can feel how it became an important part of our identity, sense of belonging, and ways of relating. We carry this role with us throughout our lives, and it translates to the persona or mask we show to the world. With this first domain of experience, which aligns with the first house in astrology, we're working with the statement "I am."

So: How *do* you come across when you first meet others? Are you the bull in the china shop? Do you come in loudly and demand attention? Do you enter reservedly and meekly and test the waters? Are you always looking for ways to be helpful to others? Or are you trying to impress people? So many of us have been raised to believe that looking good is enough, but is it really? Are you one of those *very put-together* people? Or do you come in with your freak flag flying? Each of these first impressions relates to the balance of elements in your fundamental makeup.

The first impression we make is enormously significant. Research shows that within the first minute or so of meeting someone in a job interview, at a gathering, or on a date, our brains are firing millions of bits of information to put that person in some kind of category of likes and dislikes, and to instruct us to move away or move toward.

A client once said to me that one of her worst fears was being judged when she walked into a room. I said, "Well, that's an accurate fear, because everyone is judging everyone the minute they show up." It is not a bad thing! In order for our species to survive, each of us had to develop antennae to see who's with us, who could be dangerous, who we know to approach with gentleness or caution. Everybody's judging everyone all the time, and as long as we recognize that this is what we're doing, it's okay.

But guess who we're most preoccupied with judging? That's right, ourselves. I would say it's an 80/20 proposition: 80 percent of most people's attention is on how they're coming across, and their own self-reflection, while 20 percent goes to how other people are occurring to them. Once we relax with the idea that judging is just an instinctual sorting system, we do not have to try to remove it or shame the judge in our mind. Real maturity comes in when we realize that our prejudgments of people are inherently flawed and unfair, and that we should proceed with actual curiosity and the willingness to learn something entirely different about someone than what we first assume. An awareness of personas and masks gives us many opportunities to question our prejudices and to better understand and forgive the prejudices of others.

The inventories that follow are designed to support you in assessing the balance of elemental energies that creates your default self-presentation and persona. They will give you a clearer picture of the energy you bring when you enter a room, and will reveal to you some of your predispositions and patterns—possibly showing you things you've never thought about before, and thus helping expand your repertoire. They will assist you in evaluating the impact of those energies on how you naturally occur to others, and build on the weaker energies in a way that utilizes all your strengths while promoting some of your less developed sides.

Assessment: Role Play

What were your assigned roles or qualities in your family of origin? Check or circle all that are true.

Fire

☐ Clown

☐ Bad boy/bad girl

☐ Bold

☐ Selfish

☐ Athlete

☐ Autonomous

☐ Creative

☐ Entertainer

☐ Truth-teller

☐ Angry

☐ Religious

☐ Seeker

Earth

- [ ] Good girl/good boy
- [ ] Helper
- [ ] Hero
- [ ] Achiever
- [ ] Self-reliant
- [ ] Practical
- [ ] Loser
- [ ] Materialistic
- [ ] Caretaker

Air

- [ ] Peacekeeper
- [ ] Rebel
- [ ] Thinker
- [ ] Scared
- [ ] Airhead
- [ ] Weirdo
- [ ] Talker
- [ ] Mediator
- [x] Outgoing
- [x] Friendly
- [ ] Brilliant

Water

- [ ] Scapegoat
- [ ] Sensitive
- [ ] Dreamer
- [ ] Quiet
- [ ] Feeler
- [ ] Secretive
- [ ] Patient
- [ ] Addictive
- [ ] Codependent
- [ ] Safe
- [ ] The big crier
- [ ] Intense
- [ ] Sexual
- [ ] Spiritual
- [ ] Crazy

After completing this assessment, notice what elements have the most checked or circled qualities/roles. This will reflect well the persona you carry and the mask you wear; in astrology, it will probably correlate well with the meaning of your rising sign and/or any planets in your first house.

Role Play: Practice

Sit down with a trusted other and talk about the role you were unconsciously cast to play in your family. How do you feel about it today? Or, if you feel like investigating this topic in a more solitary way, journal, write a poem, or create a piece of visual art as you reflect.

Assessment: Unmask Yourself

What is someone's impression when they first meet you? What adjective would they use to describe you? Circle or check all those that are true. Then go back through and mark those you would *like* to be true but didn't circle or check.

Fire

- ☐ Charismatic
- ☐ Magnetic
- ☐ Bold
- ☐ Enthusiastic
- ☐ Audacious
- ☐ Brash

- ☒ Blunt
- ☐ Intense
- ☐ Outrageous
- ☐ Intimidating

Earth

- ☐ Solid
- ☐ Centered
- ☐ Calm
- ☑ Steady
- ☐ Stodgy
- ☐ Thick
- ☐ Stubborn
- ☐ Critical
- ☐ Competitive

Air

- ☐ Electrifying
- ☐ Captivating
- ☐ Enthralling
- ☐ Inspiring
- ☐ Flighty
- ☐ Distracted
- ☐ Insincere
- ☐ Unemotional
- ☐ Distant
- ☐ Chatty

Water

- ☐ Alluring
- ☐ Mesmerizing
- ☐ Seductive
- ☐ Comforting
- ☐ Kind
- ☐ Mushy
- ☐ Spineless
- ☐ Blubbery
- ☐ Slippery
- ☐ Deceivable

ILLUMINATIONS

"I am" is the key phrase for the first astrological house. Planets in this house introduce you to others without you doing anything.

Even if your first house is empty of planets, the rising sign still puts something forward. If you know your rising sign, you can learn about the *you* that people first encounter by finding it in this list of "I am . . ." statements:

Aries: I am bold.

Taurus: I am beautiful.

Gemini: I am a communicator.

Cancer: I am a nurturer.

Leo: I am a performer.

Virgo: I am a helper.

Libra: I am a harmonizer.

Scorpio: I am a prober.

Sagittarius: I am positive.

Capricorn: I am accomplishing.

Aquarius: I am friendly.

Pisces: I am sensitive.

Having planets in the first house will enhance and color the impact of this first impression. For example: My friend has Leo rising but no planets in her first house. She has many of those creative, expressive, loving Leo qualities, but might have expressed them more fully or along added dimensions if she also had planets in her first house. And although I'm a receptive, open, optimistic, dorky kind of person with adventurous, outgoing, celebratory Sagittarius rising, having Saturn and Mars in my first house has created a pattern where people who don't yet know me feel scared of and intimidated by me. I always have to apologize for this at some point.

The words "I am" have a great deal of power. I learned a great exercise of saying twenty-five "I am . . ." statements a day about my positive qualities—"I am kind," "I am gracious," and so on—and to also state twenty "I am . . ." positive phrases about my body—"I am beautiful," "I am ageless," "I am smooth," and so on. Knowing about the archetypes represented by my rising sign and the planets in the first house of my chart helps me create statements that really ring true, but I can craft them easily around any positive quality I can own about myself. If I can spot it, I've got it, and I expand it by naming it.

This exercise is powerful! Within thirty days, I noticed an incredible uptick in my personal magnetism and manifestation powers. Try it!

Unmask Yourself: Practices

1. Show a close someone the preceding list of qualities. Ask them to share which of these characteristics they noticed about you when you first met. What other qualities do they see now that they know you well?

2. Go back through the lists a second time. What qualities, roles, or personas would you like to play with that you did *not* circle or check? What roles do you want to incorporate more into your identity? Consider especially the element categories where you circled or checked the fewest roles. How can you integrate these into your persona and presentation? Talk, write, or create around these aspirations.

Making Impressions

When my own adult daughter was young, she had this narrative going that people were scared of her. Her rising sign or ascendant—the sign that rules the first house or domain of experience—is a water sign, Scorpio, which tends to be furtive, secretive, cautious, and suspicious.

Once she did more personal growth work around this feeling that people were scared of her, she realized that she was putting out a vibe of "I don't trust you, I don't want to get close to you, I'm suspicious of you," which others met with hesitancy and caution. But once she saw that her chart had fire and air elements to draw on, she started tempering the suspicion and mistrust with a lot of joy and energy (fire) and curiosity (air) when meeting other people.

As she developed in her life, she became quite a gifted yoga teacher, public speaker, and actor. From there, she realized that she could use her water intensity to really connect with people, alongside a sense of joyful, honest creativity. And now, she's a wildly beloved teacher who can draw on her personal experience of hesitancy and timidity to help others feel very safe in their concerns about getting to know people.

A colleague of mine has a very strong earth chart, but her first house or domain is ruled by the element fire. With Leo rising, she had a role of joy bringer and creative spark in her family of origin, but she was also brought up to be highly responsible and dutiful. There was always a sense that she was supposed to bring the fun and exuberance, but it felt tamped down by what

Brené Brown calls "foreboding joy": a sense that one shouldn't let oneself get too carried away with the abandon of wild happiness. One shouldn't be *out of control* because mistakes could be made, and mistakes could hurt others or bring shame to oneself. So that loving, abundant, creative, joyful spark of the fire in her first domain wasn't really coming through. Unless she was performing (and she did become a performer—this was her main expression of Leo rising), she was reserved and tamped down.

She recognized that this didn't feel true to her sense of "I am," so she started working on bringing out the exquisite, uninhibited, spontaneous gestural and facial expressiveness of fire in her everyday life and relationships. She became more animated and able to mirror other people incredibly well, through a lens of sparky, playful, frisky joy. Sure enough, all of her relationships became more enchanted and animated, which led her to deeper work about not having felt seen or welcomed by parents, who couldn't handle the true dimensions of her fire.

A friend of mine has Capricorn rising. The role she was given in her family was to look respectable, to seem to know what was going on, and to be reliable, punctual, and authoritative. The message she got was that she could never make a mistake and had to enter every situation having it all together. This caused my friend great distress in groups and social settings, because she had an internal message that she could never really relax fully into being herself. As she worked with this earth-element rising of dutiful obedience, she realized that she could become her own best source of authority and self-approval. She was able to calm others' social fears by feeling okay herself. She started trusting that her genuine, spontaneous self was her best source of social authenticity and confidence. As everyone experiences some kind of insecurity in social meetings or work settings, she saw how simply showing up in this way could help many others feel respected and like they belong.

Another friend of mine has Gemini, an air sign, rising. Air-rising people are very good at conversation, taking things out of thin air and making small talk, and being able to converse about a variety of subjects. They have a lot of curiosity, but they have not always learned that brevity is social charity, and sometimes they come across as airheads or know-it-alls who habitually talk over people. And so this friend started really investigating, listening more than talking, and getting much more concrete about what they wanted to say. They had to use the earth element to bring those high, lofty, abstract conversations down into practical and listenable nuggets. Once they started narrowing things down and bringing concepts into an earthier plane, they noticed that more people were attracted to spending time with them. They had been unconsciously dominating conversations with a lot of ideas but not much connection. Now, they could have truly meaningful conversations that felt connecting and satisfying to everyone involved.

One of my friends has Scorpio rising, and within the first minute of meeting up with her, I know whether our time together is going to be a deeply engaging, authentic conversation or a dark, bloody dive into her suffering. Another of my friends has Aquarius rising, and I know she is always going to be friendly and a bit eccentric; but in the first minute, I can tell whether she is going to come from a diffuse, expansive Aquarian airiness, or from a space of being more focused on a certain cause.

Confidence versus Conformity

Many of my clients express the desire for more self-confidence when they enter a room. They have big fears that the first impressions they make are inadequate or unacceptable. People want to feel more assured about their personal social style. So, what is confidence, anyway? It is a self-trust and self-acceptance that means you are good with who you are, inside and out. It is the opposite of seeking approval and evaluating every step based on other people's values or judgments.

What stops most of us from feeling self-confident—choosing, instead, to conform, even when it doesn't feel true to who we are—is the fear of being negatively judged or rejected. As I said earlier in this chapter, the fear of being judged is based on the fact that *everyone is judging everyone, all of the time*. We judge others and we judge ourselves. That's basically what our thinking brains are built to do: your brain, my brain, the brain of the person you're worried is making up something negative about you. Knowing this, we can begin to choose not to let the fear of judgment dictate who we show up to be.

Another layer of challenge is that a self-protective part of our brain (a reactive, emotional part called the *amygdala*) is supersensitive to the possibility of being rejected by others.

Historically, conformity has been enforced by truly dangerous and damaging consequences, like being cast out or severely punished for having beliefs or behaviors that don't mesh with the expectations of the dominant culture. (And it continues to be physically dangerous to be oneself in some parts of the world, or if one is part of a group that experiences oppression and harm.) That self-protective part can cause us to unconsciously revert to conformity in order to protect ourselves from the pain of rejection.

If you have the privilege of knowing that your physical or mental well-being is not truly threatened by what other people think of you, you can work on noticing where you are being what others think you should be rather than bringing your true personal magnetism to whatever space you're in. Notice whether you're coming from your heart or from your amygdala. As you learn to discern between coming from love or coming from fear, you can begin to focus on the way you *want* to impact and interact with others.

The next level of greater self-confidence has to do with deciding how you want to make others feel. Once you've released yourself from the fear of being judged, you can consider: *what impact do you want to have on others?*

When we enter the room caught up in wondering what others think about us, we lose or dilute our personal magnetism. Creating great moments for *others* in every interaction is not that hard to do if you focus on bringing out the best in them instead of trying to contort yourself to be what you imagine they want you to be.

A first step toward greater self-confidence is recognizing your natural social style, which is reflected by the element of your rising sign or the elements that were most prominent in the role play assessment. Knowing the style you tend to default to—for example, if you have a water rising sign (Cancer, Pisces, or Scorpio), you may be a bit shy when you first meet people—you can begin to be more purposeful about bringing other energies in to balance or replace the shyness.

The reward for conformity is that everyone likes you but yourself.

–Rita Mae Brown (she has the Sun and Mars oppose the independence-seeking Uranus)

To continue with this example, acknowledging and accepting this persona or mask as natural to you, you can go on to consider qualities you wish to express more when making a first impression. Perhaps you can set an intention to bring a calm and supportiveness that makes others feel socially and emotionally safe. Holding this intention will help you put all your nervous energy into helping others be more relaxed and listened to.

You've got this!

Onward . . .

Being aware of how you impact others the minute you walk into a room, you can take that extra moment to work with yourself before seeing someone. When you set the frame for your best to shine through, it will certainly enhance any room you walk into.

Start to take a moment before you meet up with people to

breathe fully and to decide how you want to show up. Remember: folks get a snapshot of you in the first sixty seconds of their encounter with you, even if they know you well. How do you want to be seen? Think this through beforehand. Be present to the difference it makes.

With your expanded awareness of the first impression you tend to make, think about how it differs from what you consider your "real self" to be. You might begin to help others see that real self more quickly and clearly by filling in the blanks: "People tend to first see me as _____. When they get to know me better, they see my _____ side. If I intentionally bring my qualities of _____, _____, and _____, people can get to know the real me faster." (Bonus points for including qualities reflective of elements that balance the one that rules your rising sign!)

Remember: You are not only the mask you wear! Your persona is the face you show to the world, and it does not at all convey the depth of who you are and who you might be. This is why we can discover new ways to show up—new masks to wear—and experiment with our personas as playfully and seriously as we played characters in our childhood games of pretend.

CHAPTER TWO

The Second Domain:
Your Core Values and Worth

The second domain is about *what you have* and how secure you feel in your ability to keep it and make it grow. Some of what we have is material: houses, cars, books, works of art, clothes, devices. Some of what we have is intangible: self-esteem, relationships with ourselves and others, beauty, practices, vocations, vacations.

Living this domain fully is about knowing your worth. The first step is to get clear about what you value. When you take the time and put in the work to identify your core values, you can intentionally create a life that fulfills them—including the material and immaterial things that bring you contentment and joy. When you stick to your values no matter how tempted you are to veer away from them, you will know just what to acquire, what to hold on to, and what to let go of, and you will develop a rock-hard sense of self-worth.

Acquisition and consumption are momentary pleasures that all too often lead us straight into wanting something else we don't yet have. Once we have obtained necessities like housing, food, and healthcare, there is absolutely no correlation between more things and more happiness. The work of this domain (and of the second astrological house) is cherishing what you do have, conserving your precious energy, and not overextending energetically or financially.

Our culture is obsessed with unlimited growth and expansion to the point of killing our resources and exhausting everyone's adrenal systems. The human ego keeps wanting more and more, no matter what we have; yet, at the soul level, *having* more and more can be a major distraction from what brings us the most meaning, pleasure, and contentment. In my astrology practice, I've worked with dozens of billionaires; through the nonprofit I cofounded, I've worked with hundreds of folks at the other end of the socioeconomic spectrum. I can confidently state that there is no difference whatsoever between the haves and the have-nots regarding self-esteem—which happens to be the deepest issue of this second domain.

I'm not here to talk you out of acquiring things that bring you joy, but I do want to make a distinction between the joy that comes from acquisition and the joy that comes from living in accordance with our most deeply held values. These kinds of joy are not mutually exclusive, but the latter kind requires much deeper work. What we own and what we have matter most as reflections of the values we hold.

The most contented people I know are the ones who understand that the most important things they possess are their intimate and authentic connections with others. Spiritually speaking, who we really are has nothing to do with the money in our bank account, our beauty, or our possessions; it has everything to do with how truly loved we feel and how fully expressed our stable intimate connections are. At the end of life, no one is touting how much they earned, how many cars they drove, or even how great their body looked. Most often, they reflect on how they loved and were loved.

✦

ILLUMINATIONS

"I have" is the key phrase for this second domain, which represents the second house in astrology. The second house has traditionally been related to money and what one owns, and the signs associated with planets in this house (or the sign that rules this house if no planets reside there in your natal chart) have been used to explore the potentials and problems we might experience in our material lives. It's true that the planets you have in the second house and their relationships with other planets in your birth chart (their *aspects;* see page 227 in Appendix 1) will point to how you grapple with the sometimes messy business of stuff and money, and a broader view will give you information about how you can apply your values in ways that bring in the stuff and money you desire.

The sign you find on the second-house cusp can yield insights about the issues you have to work on regarding your self-worth. (A cusp is the part of the chart that demarcates one domain from another. The second-house cusp therefore is the very edge and beginning of the area defined as the second house.) For example, if you have Capricorn on the second-house cusp, your work here is around your need to impress others and constantly earn approval in order to have even a momentary sense of being enough. If you recognize that this is your default and notice where you are relying too much on externally endowed gold stars for work well done, you can learn to acknowledge your own excellence and success based on how well you live out and act on your core values.

Planets in the second house yield information about things you are highly attached to and ways you can bring resources to your life. Having Mercury in your natal second house indicates that the mind and communications are highly important to you, and that you can open up your flow of resources through stellar writing or speaking.

Whatever resources you *do* have are foundations to attract other resources. Venus in the second house, for example, indicates that you have resources of love and beauty that can help you attract other things, like networks and contacts. It might also help you land a beautiful partner.

Assessment: Your Treasure Chest

Scan these lists for the top five values you hold most dear today. Pick the ones you could not live without, knowing that the rest are important, too. Mark each of them with a circle or check mark. Then draw a line through the three values that feel *least* important to you.

Fire

- ☐ Adventure
- ☐ Honesty
- ☐ Innovation
- ☐ Change
- ☐ Passion
- ☐ Creativity
- ☐ Spontaneity
- ☐ Aliveness
- ☐ Courage

Earth

- ☐ Integrity
- ☐ Steadiness
- ☐ Calm
- ☐ Reliability
- ☐ Security
- ☐ Practicality
- ☐ Loyalty
- ☐ Time in nature
- ☐ Presence
- ☐ Commitment

Air

- ☐ Liveliness
- ☐ Communication
- ☐ Freedom
- ☐ Openness
- ☐ Intelligence
- ☐ Inspiration
- ☐ Brilliance
- ☐ Humor
- ☐ Learning
- ☐ Community

Water

- ☐ Empathy
- ☐ Connection
- ☐ Understanding
- ☐ Love
- ☐ Nurturing
- ☐ Kindness
- ☐ Spirituality
- ☐ Feeling
- ☐ Vulnerability
- ☐ Depth

YOUR TREASURE CHEST: PRACTICES

1. Rate yourself from 1 to 10: How consistently do you stick to the five core values you chose? What and who helps you maintain your commitment to them? Who and what contributes to you sabotaging your values? Discuss, journal, or make art around these questions.

2. Look at the three values you rated least important. These are what we call your *shadow values*. Psychologically speaking, the shadow values hold a lot of potential for you because you have not recognized them as important. The more work we put into honoring those least acknowledged values, the more whole a person we become. Discuss, journal, or make art around how you can honor those values more in your life.

Assessment: Your Strengths and Resources

Whether you face issues around not having enough or of having too much, one of the most important self-evaluations in this book focuses on assessing what you actually *do* have and how to make the most of it. This includes material, spiritual, and physical resources.

Go through these lists associated with the strengths in the four elements and circle those you currently have. On a second pass, underline all the resources you wish you had, but don't currently possess.

Fire

Strengths/Resources

Sports

Self-determination

Positive body image

Self-confidence

Public speaking

Great posture

Creative talents

Creative outlets

Consistent affection

Play and recreation habits

Great relationships with
children

Great friends

Group memberships

Community activism

Rewarding community
affiliations

Personal authenticity

Foreign travel

 Earth

Strengths/Resources

Money

Earning power

Assets

Valuable collections

Financial security

Beautiful singing or
speaking voice

Health

Contemplative practices

Mentors

Healers

Pets

Therapists

Devotional practices

Clean eating and drinking

Access to healthcare

Personal power

Retirement savings

Solid personal reputation

Solid professional
reputation

Highly disciplined

Satisfying career

Punctuality

Established legacy

Funeral plot

 Air

Strengths/Resources

Networks

Contacts

Communication skills

Transportation

Good memory

Ability to learn new things

Reading

Writing

Clean air

Phone/Internet

Close siblings

Partner

Attractiveness

Surrounded by beauty

Great style

Social equity

Wardrobe

Foreign languages

Foreign homes

International travel

Organized belief system

Access to higher
    education

Religious or spiritual
    teacher

 Water

Strengths/Resources

Home

Real estate

A close family

Living parents

Ancestral wisdom

Clean food

Safe neighborhood

Healthy sexual life

Inheritance

Saved money

Emotional honesty and
    intimacy

Ability to interpret dreams

Faith

Musical appreciation	Clean water
Musical skills	Quiet time
Psychic skills	Privacy
Empathy	Lucid dreaming
Spiritual belonging	

YOUR STRENGTHS AND RESOURCES: PRACTICES

1. Write about or discuss with a loved one the resources and strengths you identified. How are they expressed in your life? In which element are you strongest and most resourced right now?

2. Write about or discuss with a loved one the resources and strengths you would like to have more of. Focus on the elements where you circled the fewest items. What can you do to express them more strongly? How will this help to enhance your joy and contentment?

Although I made a big point from the beginning of this chapter about the second domain not being *only* about money, the truth is that it is *also* about money. To be a raging second domain financial success, you need all four elements:

Fire: Making money and accruing resources requires initiative, agency, and boldness.

Earth: Managing resources wisely means living within your means and taking impeccable care of your things, no matter how many things you have. Manifestation (see page 46) has everything to do with effort and grit. Work-averse people—often, those who are naturally endowed with lots of air and water, but very little earth or fire—will need to bolster these elements to realize their dreams.

Air: In order to earn what you deserve and create a life of abundance, you need a can-do mindset, saturated with gratitude for all those who help you get where you want to go. You need to believe it to make it happen. You need to create and access connections and networks to realize your financial dreams.

Water: To realize your worth, you need to be emotionally connected to others and to feel as much excitement about their success as you do about your own. I have not met a person with great wealth who feels rich inside without true intimacy, which is the gold standard of worthiness. Feeling truly close to others means feeling like a part of their success, and this pays itself forward to even more folks . . . and back to ourselves.

ILLUMINATIONS

If you know the astrological sign on your second-house cusp, you can leverage its wisdom to help you create resources and lasting value.

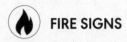 **FIRE SIGNS**

Aries: Be bold and entrepreneurial while also being gracious and diplomatic.

Leo: Use your excessive charm and creativity to get what you want while being incredibly loving to those who help you along the way.

Sagittarius: Use your positive, free, loving spirit to make acquisition and security an adventure.

 ## EARTH SIGNS

Taurus: Be as generous as you are grabby! Focus on cherishing each and every success with humility.

Virgo: Use your natural analytic mindset and service orientation to find resources that have longevity and that are helpful to others.

Capricorn: Exercise your exceptional practicality to attract wealth and influence. Remember to use these assets to nourish yourself and others.

 ## AIR SIGNS

Gemini: Use excellent communication skills to earn significant income, and assist you in connecting with networks of folks who can lift your spirits and sense of meaning.

Libra: Practice diplomacy and your way with beauty to promote your abilities to attain wealth, both financially and socially.

Aquarius: Activate community love as your greatest resource. Tap into the wellspring of diversity within the organizations and friendships in your life, and resources and affection will become more available to you.

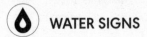 **WATER SIGNS**

Cancer: Nurture others and take care of resources in a manner that fuels your bank account. Engaging your emotional intelligence is key to creating the security you desire.

Scorpio: Utilize your investigative, surgical mindset and go behind the scenes to find out where you can make deep investments. Remember not to sting anyone, including yourself, as you accrue your stash.

Pisces: Enlarge your capacity for big dreams and visions and leverage your charisma to land enormous sums of money. Make sure you do not get lost in the dream; find others who can help you nail down details and practical applications.

Second Domain Mastery: Manifestation

When we align ourselves with our core values, identify our desires, and consciously work to balance the elements in this domain, a magnetic force of creation develops. This is the key to manifestation.

Here are seven steps to manifest what you desire:

1. Identify your core values: for example, love, honesty, or joy.
2. Name a new resource you desire: for example, a new close friend (a powerful emotional resource) or a new place to live.

3. Live from love, honesty, and joy as you make efforts to find a new close friend or new home.

4. Ask for help from your sacred circle and ask them to keep you accountable to both your values and your efforts.

5. Every day, thank the divine for its assistance.

6. Every day, express gratitude for every sign of progress toward fulfilling your desire for this new resource.

7. When you have gained the desired outcome—for example, your new friend or your new apartment—acknowledge this to yourself and to others. Pay the good energy forward by helping someone else to fulfill their desires.

This formula is reliable as long as you give it consistent effort. Don't fixate on how long it takes for what you desire to appear. All things you truly desire and make consistent efforts toward will either come to you or stop being relevant in time. Some of the things I desperately wanted years ago seem incredibly empty and foolish to me now. Desperation signals to you and others that you are trying to fill a hole. Holes attract dirt, not gold.

What do you want to manifest? Walk yourself through the steps of the practices described in the previous section. Dive deep and identify three values from which you want to dream something into being. Name the thing you wish to create. Allow the elements to fuel your journey, taking time to be present to each: let yourself feel the fire of actualization; the pragmatic, grounded, logistic qualities of earth; the visioning and communication powers of air, and the emotions you will feel—the element of water—once you have made your vision a reality.

Here's a true story of manifestation from my own life. My partner and I watched an incredible documentary called *The Social Dilemma,* which our friends had produced. It was about the terrible damage being done to the fabric of our society by social media and screen addiction. The film was deeply disturbing. I felt great despair after watching it, but instead of simmering in that despair, I took it as a nudge toward social action.

Three of my core values are love, community, and nature. Guided by those values, I came up with an idea for a community event focused on love and set in nature: a digital cleanse program in Santa Barbara, where we live. Teens and adults could spend several device-free days in a beautiful natural setting, participating together in lots of creative, active, mindful, connecting activities. The key to any great idea becoming reality is to enlist support and encouragement, so I decided to pitch the idea to my colleagues at AHA!, the nonprofit where I work. People were on board and excited.

The next step was figuring out where to hold what was turning out to be a five-day event, and also to determine how we could fund such a big endeavor. Every morning, I wrote to my divine angels and guides and asked for guidance and help. I kept visualizing the event and feeling what it would be like to actually have it. Meanwhile, my partner and I researched places that might work. We decided to visit El Capitan Canyon, because it was near enough and provided cabins in a natural setting. After an amazing visit there, I put down the deposit, trusting that I would be able to secure funding for underserved youth at low cost. Then I took the bold and joyful step of asking many people I know if they would be interested in sponsoring this type of event.

This part is always scary. Asking is so vulnerable. Over decades of asking, I have learned that being a good asker means being absolutely okay with whatever answer I receive, whether a yes or a no. I have received many more noes in this lifetime than yeses. This has never stopped me, because I've found that a single yes among a thousand noes is all that's needed to manifest an important dream into reality. And it happened here: one person came through with enough to provide the scholarships needed.

Note that all of this took place during the winter Covid surge in 2021, when it felt at times as though group activities would never be possible again. I kept blessing the divine and thanking angels and friends for seeing this vision with me, even as we also all did everything we could to stay safe and stop the spread of Covid-19. Gratitude for each new affirmation of this project lived in me every day, and I spoke it aloud to my partner and friends. My vision of the digital cleanse was a bright light at the end of the long, dark tunnel of the pandemic—but I had no idea how long that tunnel would turn out to be when I chose the dates and put down the deposit. In April 2021, we hit the next Covid safety tier, and we were able to open applications to the AHA! Digital Cleanse.

I never lost my faith during this process, and I also con-stantly surrendered control of timing and outcomes. I held to my values of love, community, and nature every day while doing as much as humanly possible to usher this vision into reality. My values led me to a creative vision, which then—through great support from my sacred crew, my own unwavering perseverance, and divine grace—became real.

Onward . . .

Each morning, before you start your day, state your intention to live from your most precious values. Take active steps and marshal support from your close loved ones. When called to take a risk to move the ball forward, ask those beloveds to help you intuit whether the risk is worth it. Know that sometimes the outcome of a risky move is impossible to predict, and that it will come down to a leap of faith. The universe appreciates such leaps when you soar off the precipice with clarity about your vision and your values. My experience has been that she tends to provide a delightfully soft landing when she knows we are being true to ourselves and to the gifts we wish to give the world. At every increment of manifestation, thank the divine for its support. Watch magic unfold.

CHAPTER THREE

The Third Domain:
How You Speak and Listen

In this chapter, our focus will be on communication: How do you speak? How do you listen? The most influential and self-realized people I know are great at both. No matter what sign is on your third-house cusp, or what sign the planet of Mercury is in, you can learn to communicate using all four elements. Indeed, the most accomplished communicators I know can mirror all four elements when listening to others, and can tailor their speaking to the element needed.

We are always communicating—both nonverbally and verbally—and often, we don't really know how we are being received. Too often we are expecting people to "get" us without really bothering to understand how they process communication and how they best understand messages that are being sent. We do not all have the same styles of expression. If we are to be stellar interactors, we need to work on expanding our style to match the styles of others instead of wishing that each person would just see the light and conform to our style.

ILLUMINATIONS

Here are some basic communication tips based on the sign ruling your third house:

Aries: Slow down! Speaking is not a competition or sport. Use your boldness to be kind and protective.

Taurus: Speed up! Taking your time to get to your point is one thing, but other people want to stay awake for the ride. Use your sensual grasp of communication to be clear and concise.

Gemini: Keep to one topic at a time. Take pauses to see if others are with you. Instead of monologuing, ask more excellent questions.

Cancer: Use your emotional responsiveness to speak to people's strengths rather than coddling or mothering them.

Leo: Be dramatic and affectionate in your speech . . . yet also host the radiance and specialness of others. Yes, it's all about *you,* but it's also all about *them.*

Virgo: You are a master communicator of details. Don't get lost in small chunks or bits of data.

Libra: Use your exquisite diplomatic skills to shine the light on others, yet don't forget that your opinion matters, too.

Scorpio: You will be able to dig under any surface with your probing questions and attentive listening. Resist any impulse to use your laser-like communication skills to shame or blame.

Sagittarius: Your joy and directness are your superpowers. But remember that bluntness is not a good strategy.

Capricorn: You are great at getting to the bottom line and keeping things real. Don't forget to give people some grace in their need to spin a tale.

Aquarius: Your aerial view of things helps knit pieces together. Don't be so "out there" that no one can follow you.

Pisces: Your empathy is fabulous and your sensitivity is needed. Remember that communications conveying self-pity and victimhood are not your best moves.

As an astrologer, I notice how often people miss each other in terms of how they express themselves. For example: Nisha talks in stories and circles. She likes to roll in many fillers and pauses and enjoys passionate stream-of-consciousness musings. Her husband, Jack, speaks in declarative sentences. Jack wants earth talk; Nisha wants fireside chats. When they are working on something together, Jack gets irritated with Nisha's circumambulatory orations and Nisha feels dismissed and judged by Jack's focus on getting to the point.

Randall likes to talk about ideas and visions. He is the ultimate air-element skywriter who sees the big picture and can wax on about pies in the sky for a long time. His partner, Tim, likes to get to the heart of the subject. He wants to consider what things will *feel* like and likes to mull over the connections be-tween people—how they will all feel when they work together on something. Randall ends up feeling invalidated and Tim ends up feeling brushed off and judged as oversensitive.

In both of these relationship dynamics, the participants are leaning into judgment rather than curiosity. Curiosity is proba-bly the single most important tool in communication. True cu-riosity always coexists with openness, and if I am open, I can meet anyone where they are. Rumi wrote, "Out beyond ideas of wrongdoing and right doing, there is a field. I'll meet you there."

In every group I have ever led, people have expressed the desire to be heard without judgment. The funny thing is that the mind is a judgment-making machine. There's no controlling its automatic tendency to judge. What people really want, I think, is to be *heard* by people who might have all kinds of judgments flying around in their minds, but who don't let those judgments get in the way of truly listening and being present.

Let's say I am talking with my friend Melissa about her son Bo. She tells me he's lied again to her about his grades. She's really upset. In my mind, I think, *Bo. That kid. He is such a shit to her, and I hate him for that.* I notice that, but what I say when I open my mouth is "Ugh! That sounds frustrating! Tell me what it's like for you."

She goes on to say that yes, she is totally frustrated, and also hurt. "I want things to be different," she says.

My mind says, *Bo will never change.* What my mouth says is "How can I support you with this?"

I have learned the hard way to not do other people's inventories for them, because it just becomes a drain of my energy. Every time I want to solve someone else's life I ask myself, *What advice do I need to heed for myself?* If someone specifically asks me what I think they should do, I'll do my best to give them something good, but *no one* likes receiving unsolicited advice.

It's easy to mistake our judgments of others for advice we need to give. Even if a just-right answer were to come from me in response to Melissa, it would lack impact because it didn't come from within her—and might alienate her from me when what she needs most is to connect. I can trust her to know her own best answers.

Assessment: So You Say

Communication is fundamental to our happiness, our success, and even our survival. Great communication consists of intending a certain message and then having that exact message be received and understood.

In the following lists, circle or check all the sentence completions that are true for you.

Fire

I speak

- ☐ directly
- ☐ honestly
- ☐ immediately
- ☐ passionately
- ☐ bravely
- ☐ truth to power
- ☐ insensitively
- ☐ without waiting for others to finish
- ☐ combatively

☐ angrily

☐ over people

☐ I say it the way it is

Earth

I speak

☐ slowly

☐ thoughtfully

☐ specifically

☐ cautiously

☐ practically

☐ coherently

☐ sensuously

☐ turgidly

☐ repetitively

☐ in a monotone

☐ critically

☐ I like to get right to the point

Air

I speak

☐ abstractly

☐ logically

☐ fairly

☐ openly

☐ inspirationally

☐ radically

☐ intellectually

☐ objectively

☐ arrogantly

☐ disconnectedly

☐ obscurely

☐ incessantly

☐ in an ungrounded way

Water

I speak

☐ softly

☐ kindly

☐ compassionately

☐ empathetically

☐ lovingly

☐ endearingly

☐ powerfully   ☐ from a wounded place

☐ with feeling   ☐ pitifully

☐ avoidantly   ☐ from a disempowered

☐ nastily   place

☐ like a victim

Notice the element under which you circled the most qualities of communication.

Go back and underline a few qualities that you would like to bring more into your style of speaking, writing, and otherwise reaching out to connect with others through words. Start by making a list of five new qualities you would like to integrate into your communication style. Carry this list with you and each day make an intention to work on those qualities. At the end of the day check off which qualities you did indeed utilize.

SO YOU SAY: PRACTICE

1. Bravely ask three people in your life for their candid assessment of your communication style. Deeply listen to them as they share about how you come across.

2. In your day-to-day life, consciously and intentionally tap into the communication qualities you underlined in the assessment.

Listening

The third domain requires equal focus on speaking and listening. In forty years of training counselors and teaching educators and staff how to listen, I've found that most of us see ourselves as pretty good listeners even when we need some work on this skill. Here are the most common ways we think we're listening well, but we're in fact doing something else.

Fire elements tend to *go to toxic positivity* **instead of deeply listening.** Sally is talking to me about how heartbroken she is over the betrayal of her partner of two years. I say, "Look . . . you know you're better off without him. Just focus on all the good things you have going for you . . . you'll feel better faster if you only look at the bright side." Again, this intervention is not awful, it's just not deep listening. I'm trying to make Sally feel better, partly so that I can avoid sitting with her in her pain.

If I have a lot of fire, this strategy of burning quickly through painful emotions might feel natural to me, but when I assume the same about others, they can end up not feeling heard. Empathy is what's required here to actually let Sally feel just exactly what she's feeling. I can sit in these uncomfortable feelings with her and trust that she'll find the perfect path of unwinding them toward a new life.

Earth elements tend to *give advice* **instead of deeply listening.** It can feel good to offer sage advice to someone who's sharing something meaningful with us, but what they often need even more than our brilliant guidance is true deep listening. When we give unsolicited advice, we communicate that we don't believe the other person holds the answers within them—that we believe our wisdom is more potent than their own.

Let's say Julian calls me up to talk about a real struggle dealing with his father, who keeps drunk-dialing him during work. I jump in: "Block his number. You don't have to let him have access to you anymore." And Julian gets very quiet. He respects me, so he wants to listen to me, but I've just cut off his opportunity to consider for himself how he should handle this complex issue. If what I recommend feels wrong to him, he has to decide whether to explain why; and he may be concerned that I will feel disrespected if he doesn't follow my advice. What Julian really needs is for me to listen deeply to his story and to then ask him what kinds of solutions he thinks might work best for him.

Air elements tend to *distract* instead of deeply listening. When somebody's in the middle of telling you something and you switch the topic, make a deflecting joke, look down at your phone, or drift off into your own head to construct a grocery list or remember who you need to call later, you're not present. In a world more full of distractions than ever before, this type of listening happens more frequently than any one of us would like to admit.

Water elements tend to *identify* instead of deeply listening. Zoë tells me that she's having a real issue with her stepson. "He's not listening to me," she says. "He's going out at night and not coming back till all hours . . ." I break in and blurt, "Ugh! My stepson does that, too . . . it's so aggravating . . . and there's nothing I can do to get him to stop!"

At that moment, I feel like we're really getting each other. She has an issue . . . and I have the *same issue*! But when somebody's telling their story and you break in to identify, what you're actually doing is redirecting them to listen to *your* story. You now become the subject instead of the receiver. It's not bad to identify with people when they're talking, but it's not deep listening.

How Do You Listen? Practice

Did you recognize your go-to ways of responding to others in the previous section? Are you primarily an identifier, a toxic-positivity sharer, an advice giver, or a distractor? Or do you tend to dabble in all of these responses when someone needs to be listened to?

Grab a partner for this next fun exercise. I encourage you to be super playful as you move through it; keep in mind that *everyone*, me included, will sometimes listen in these ways, and it's usually not harmful! This is just a chance for you to feel the difference between true deep listening and the kind of listening we normally encounter. Once you've done this practice, you'll have a much-heightened awareness of your choices as a listener, and you'll be clearer about how *you* most want to be listened to.

1. Choose who will share first. That person will come up with something that's been bothering them—preferably, not something too heavy.
2. The person sharing will start to talk about their situation. The listener gives them a moment, and then jumps in intentionally with an identifying statement. Let the sharer have a moment to feel what that's like. Talk about it a little.

3. As the sharer goes on with their story, blast them with some toxic positivity. As with the first round, take a minute to talk about what that feels like before moving on to advice giving and distraction.

4. Repeat with roles switched.

5. Take a few final minutes to talk about what you noticed or discovered.

True Deep Listening

Truly, deeply listening means being present to the person who's talking without any preconceived idea of what they're going to say, and without organizing yourself to respond or reply while the other person is speaking. It's a decision to be completely open and receptive to hearing this person as if for the very first time, even if it is your longtime partner or friend.

No matter what element you are naturally strong in, you can bring in the power of the other elements if being a superlative listener is impor-tant to you. When we truly, deeply listen, we call upon all four elements: Fire reflects our ability to listen with rapt attention. Earth is about hold-ing steady even as we manage big

> We think we listen, but very rarely do we listen with real understanding, true empathy. Yet listening, of this very special kind, is one of the most potent forces for change that I know.
>
> —Carl Rogers (a disciplined and committed communicator who had Sun, Moon, Mercury, and Saturn in the practical earth sign of Capricorn)

emotions. Air is about listening with cognitive empathy, which means keeping a dispassionate and even-tempered view to help coach the person toward their own understanding instead of overstepping and emotionally rescuing them. Water represents our ability to listen with empathy, and connect with the feelings of what someone is saying. This type of listening is more heart-centered and focuses on the nuances and inflections of emotional states.

Receiving and Reflecting

Deep listening means truly attending to both the *content* and the *process* of what the person is saying: both the words coming from the person's mouth (content) and their body language and emotional tone (process). As you engage deeply with all of this, set an intention to listen *responsively,* which means reflecting the content of what the person is saying as well as the feeling behind it. If Johnny says to me, "I've been struggling every single day to get up when my alarm goes off because I always have a headache," I might reflect back the content of what he's said like this: "Hmm . . . so the headaches you're experiencing are making it hard for you to wake up in the mornings." This is simply a content reflection, and this alone tends to feel very good to people. They'll show that you've understood them by nodding their heads.

Adding a process, feeling reflection weaves in the universal language of emotions, which helps folks feel even more seen and cared for. Let's say Molly is talking to me about having *so* much busywork to do, and about having her colleagues keep piling it on and then not having them respond to her after she works hard to get it done for them. I might reflect back to Molly, "Sounds like you're feeling extremely tired of people not really getting what you do . . . just unacknowledged and

> If you want to be listened to, you should put in time listening.
>
> —Marge Piercy (she has Moon and Pluto conjunct in Cancer trine Venus in Pisces)

drained." Molly nods, her body relaxes, and she knows I care about how she feels.

Another valuable listening skill is called *summarizing* or *paraphrasing*. Summarizing is what you do once you've listened for a while and have some salient chunks you can reflect back. Maybe Roxy is telling me about how her family has different real estate properties in Goleta and that each one has tenants that are not paying their rent. Roxy doesn't have any way to get that rent money paid. She's in the middle of a whole spiral of economic consequences, because she doesn't have any leeway with her creditors. If I'm going to summarize content, I don't repeat the whole thing back to her; I'm not a transcriber. What I can say to Roxy is "There's a lot of economic stress on your family right now . . . you haven't been able to collect rent, which is income you need, and there's no relief for you as a landlord in that process." Again, you'll know people feel listened to from their body language if you summarize accurately.

The most useful skill in deep listening is stillness. We often feel so much pressure to advise, comfort, change the subject, or otherwise move things along, but just holding space in stillness and listening completely is what gives the other person room to fully express themselves. Intentionally get comfortable with pauses and silence. Practice listening to understand rather than listening to reply. Notice your impulses to fill in gaps and *do something;* take a breath; and then refocus on the person to whom you're listening. Remember that when someone is quiet and fully engaged in listening to us, we feel like the center of loving attention . . . and this is a powerful healing in itself. When you want to call forth that deep quiet, think of being a vast, still lake; a majestic mountain; an enormous blue sky; or a gorgeous, peaceful campfire.

Asking open-ended questions is the final lesson of this crash course on deep listening. An open-ended question begins with "what" or "how" and cannot be answered with a simple yes or no. *What's it like for you these days to be a single parent? What do you know about addiction and how it affects families? How did your vacation go? What were the peaks and valleys?* Great listeners are authentically curious and ask lots of open-ended questions.

We've all heard the old saying about the real reason we have two ears and one mouth: because in all situations, we're meant to listen twice as much as we talk. Because I'm a professional listener, all of this is second nature to me, and that has its downside: I can count hundreds of times I've been in social situations where no one has asked me a single question. People are starved to be listened to, and when they identify me as someone who deeply listens, they start to so enthusiastically unburden themselves that they forget I'm a person too, who also needs to be listened to! You may start to notice this as you hone your listening skills. It's a small price to pay—outweighed by the rewards of moving through the world as a great listener.

Deep Listening: Practice

Sit down with a partner. Set a timer for two minutes.

One person shares about something that's going on for them: it can be challenging, or joyful, or anywhere in between. The other person's job is to simply and deeply listen and to practice reflecting, summarizing or paraphrasing, allowing for silence, and asking open-ended questions.

At the end of the two minutes, switch roles.

At the end of both shares, take a few minutes to talk together about what that was like.

ILLUMINATIONS

Mercury backtracks in its orbit—goes retrograde—three to four times a year for about three weeks at a time. This planet governs all forms of communication and travel; so, when it goes retrograde, we are all challenged to attend more carefully to every device, vehicle, and word.

Mythologically, Mercury is the trickster. During his turn inwards/backwards, we experience all types of amusing and aggravating delays and misunderstandings. This provides us with a badly needed slowing down of communication and travel. We take lightning fast, highly efficient communications and travel for granted. How entitled have we all become to think everything sent or delivered should be clear and on time?

How amazing is it that thousands of pounds of flying metal carrying hundreds of people normally work without a single hitch?

During a Mercury retrograde period, we can treat every annoying interruption in communication systems, contracts, and travel like a meditation bell: a reminder to pause, be present, and be grateful.

I have found that Mercury responds best to humble respect for the unfathomable complexity of the systems we all rely on to connect and get places. If everyone willingly did a Mercury meditation and appreciation every day during his retrograde period, we could improve and elevate our experiences of communication and transport.

Keep in mind what I call *the rule of three* during Mercury retrograde: Before sending anything out, review it three times. Check tone, content, numbers, and dates. This helps you avoid clogging up the digital superhighway with more confusion. I have actually found that this rule of three makes for a very satisfying Mercury retrograde period. It inspires me to be more conscious and appreciative of the power of words.

Some people have Mercury in retrograde in their birth charts. This represents an extra blessing and responsibility to be a thoughtful, deliberate communicator. You've come in with a calling to reflect on and refine your words. My only caution here: Don't get too lost in the mental flossing! Say it, write it, and release it.

Giving + Receiving: Creating Balance in the Domain of Communication

Now that you've considered how others receive your communication and how you listen to others, you have an idea of which element is strongest for you in this domain. For sure, having a strong lean toward one element here can be a profound source of strength. Lots of fire brings capacity for passionate, inspiring, creative communication. Those with lots of earth are usually great at grounded, calm, measured, and compassionate communication. People with lots of air tend to be incredible visionaries, thinkers, and communicators of abstract concepts. Lots of water brings gifts for communication around emotions, and the ability to deep-dive for truth and artistic inspiration.

Let's look at a few examples of real folks whose cultivation of elements outside their predominant one or several led to greater balance as well as more effective expression of their natural strengths.

Max reads voraciously, watches the news constantly, and is up-to-date on everything. But Max tends to suck all the air out of any room he's in with all his overconfidence in knowledge about what's right and what's wrong. You can hardly get a word in when Max is talking, because anything you say will be refuted by his superior knowledge. He has clearly developed the positive faculties of air, which is about networking, learning new things, and spreading information, but he has not mastered the water qualities of listening (being aware of what other people are feeling), or its earth qualities (reading others' body language while he's talking). As Max learns from significant others that they are not enjoying his pontifications, he enrolls in a communication course, where he realizes over time that what he thought was communication was essentially lecturing. Max begins to practice the art of curiosity, asking open-ended questions, and reflecting feelings and content. He consciously slows down his words so that others might truly hear what he has to say.

Barbara is constantly overtaken by her feelings when in conversation. When she feels strongly about something, she breaks down crying, is unable to continue talking, and often takes off to find a place to collapse into a fetal position. Because others don't react with anything near the depth of feeling she experiences at the drop of a hat, she feels lonely and misunderstood a lot of the time. Barbara is so easily hijacked into feeling overwhelmed that she has to learn that her feelings are not facts: the fact that she feels something doesn't mean it's true for other people—or even for herself. Her emotional self is so powerful that it can lead her to make up stories that once she is more level, she may recognize are not true. Barbara starts to do an earth practice of breathing deeply while she talks. She pauses often to center and ground herself so that waves of feeling don't overtake her. She also begins to listen more objectively so that, instead of sinking straight into the waters of what she feels, she is able to think about what people are saying and look at the ideas being presented instead of being knocked down by intense emotion. Barbara can now speak clearly even when she's crying; she's also learned to pause and gather herself so that she can feel more grounded when relating to others.

JD speaks very clearly, but can take a lot of time to get anywhere with what she's talking about. She speaks so slowly and turgidly that by the time she's finished what she has to say, even patient listeners are bored to death. Once JD realizes that her very deliberate speech has been getting in the way of folks understanding her, she takes some classes in public speaking, where she learns to be more succinct and to use more varied intonation in her speech. After a few months, JD notices that people are much more drawn to talking to her. She is now able to get her point across, and even to add some fiery flair to make it really impactful.

Doreen is a real raconteur who often takes a long route away from the center of her story. Even her digressions have digressions! She's so creative in her storytelling that although she starts out with a great audience, most folks can't keep up with her. By the time she gets to the central ring in the circus tent of her story, they've seen so many acts that they've lost interest in the main event. Once she recognizes why she tends to lose people in those moments, Doreen begins to learn the earth skill of editing herself. She practices speaking in smaller chunks, and at intervals throughout her stories, she'll check to see whether people are following her and whether they have questions or input. This whole process of balancing her fire with earth creates a nice warm place to gather rather than an uncontrolled bonfire of interwoven and exploding story lines.

Onward . . .

To enhance your ability to communicate effectively, seek to bring in the skillful energies of all four elements:

Fire: bravery, transparency, authenticity. Cultivate the fiery quality of directness with an attention to creating harmony instead of winning. Develop the ability to stay alert and engaged with another's point of view while feeling the heat of the conversation.

Earth: conciseness, equanimity, practicality. Cultivate awareness of the time you take to speak and be clear about the goal of your sharing. Learn to be both grounded and centered when you speak, and attentive to the pace and length of your sharing. Listen in a patient and stable way to others' concerns and feelings.

Air: inspiration, articulateness, clarity. Cultivate clarity and facility with vocabulary and phrasing. Work on staying on topic without too many digressions, and on learning to tolerate and celebrate various points of view. Be curious—not judgmental—about fundamental differences.

Water: safety, caring, compassion. Lead with empathy. Show a true interest in understanding the core values and feelings of the other. Refrain from overtaking communications with intense emotional reactions. Learn to use feelings as an appropriate gateway for further discussion.

CHAPTER FOUR

The Fourth Domain: Home Inside and Out

The fourth domain relates to two important focuses of the fourth house in astrology: the home you actually live in and the feelings you experience inside that home. In this chapter, you'll explore how to create a living space for yourself with intentionality around the four elements, as well as the feeling tone you live in and manifest in your home.

The fourth astrological house concerns home, family, ancestors, and sense of belonging. The sign on your fourth house describes your early influences and confers the qualities of your home and family life, and the planets in the fourth house represent issues, strengths, and areas of learning and potential growth around home and family. (If you have no planets in this house, your focus should be on the sign that sits on the house cusp—lifting those qualities to their highest expression.)

If you have Pisces on the fourth-house cusp, for example, both the positive and difficult influences of that sign— dreaminess, imagination, feeling, and magic, as well as depression, addiction, ancestral ghosts, and oversensitivity—will impact your home and family life. If Saturn sits in that house in your natal chart, you bring a major sense of responsibility to your home and family, along with trials and tribulations around issues related to belonging. Saturn in the fourth house speaks to your potential to become a true teacher of committed family values, however you define them.

The fourth domain sense of home is, in part, about the structure or shelter in which you live: the way it reflects your internal nature and mirrors the way you feel most nurtured. Does the look and spirit of your home feel true to who you are? Does it represent earth, air, fire, and water in a way that complements the elements in your birth chart? If not, what kinds of changes can you make to bring more balance? This is one question we will explore in this chapter.

This domain is about the way your home *feels*, and about the way *you* feel when you are inside it. Each home has a feeling tone, and we can be as intentional about creating the feeling tone that we want as we can be about choosing the right couch or the right art pieces for the walls.

Let's dive into the actual architecture and sensory qualities of your home. How does it reflect who you are? How does it make you feel? Are there ways you could shape or adjust details of your home to create better balance?

Your Physical Home

Can you recall times when you were traveling, or when you didn't have a choice about where you lived, and you were stuck in a place that felt utterly wrong? I've been there, and it felt like true rest was impossible—like there was an invisible friction between me and the place, or a need for me to hold up self-protective barriers. Either way, I ended up feeling drained, guarded, and on edge.

Places have their own psychology. The minute we step into someone's home, we get a gut feeling about that place. Some places are spooky. Some places are extremely relaxing or invigorating. Some places are suffocating or confining. And our individual responses to spaces can vary dramatically based on our own psychological makeup. A space that's spooky to me might feel inspiring to someone else. A space that is cozy and welcoming to you might feel closed in and airless to me. The elemental makeup of our birth charts—and whatever is going on in our fourth astrological house—can help us understand our gut reactions to different spaces, and how to shape our living environments in ways that make them feel exquisitely like home.

ILLUMINATIONS

The fourth astrological house is also associated with mothers: how we were mothered and how we mother. (Men, women, and nonbinary folks can all mother others, as can people who do not have children.) It also represents the roots we were given to support or hinder our sense of belonging and of feeling safe and nurtured.

Psychologically speaking, the fourth house reveals issues and gifts from our families of origin. It also describes who you are in your most private moments: When no one is looking and you are alone in your room, *who are you?* That most interior self is built from early family influences, and we all have influences that were helpful and others that were unhelpful.

We never truly leave our original home, where our inner characters and feeling selves were formed. We bring it with us into every other home we ever inhabit. The fourth house can grant us insights that enable us to choose whether to continue a harmful family legacy. Cultivating a physical home space that is safe and welcoming and building emotional intelligence are two important ways we can break the chains of dysfunctional family patterns.

Assessment: At Home with the Elements

It is important for your living space to send a message to the deepest, most vulnerable part of your psyche that you are safe and held, and that you can relax. With this in mind, look at these lists reflective of fire, earth, air, and water structures or houses, and go through them three times:

1. On your first pass, underline characteristics that describe your current home environment.

2. The second time, notice whether there are any characteristics you wish your home had, but doesn't. Circle them.

3. Go back one more time and notice whether there are characteristics you would like less of or would like to get rid of altogether. Cross them out.

Throughout this activity, hold in your mind and heart your innermost soul longing around the type of structure that would make you feel most at home.

 Fire environments

Dramatic	Over the top
Colorful	Clashing
Playful	Intense
Statement pieces	Large, bold art pieces
Fire features	Hunter trophies
Red	Lots of pictures of yourself
Orange	Chaotic
Yellow	Cluttered

 Earth environments

Made of wood or clay	Cavelike
Earth tones	In a rugged or natural
Furnished with found or	setting
natural elements	On a mountain
Textured rugs	Solid construction
Cozy	Durable

Sustainable materials	Dark
Smothering	Cloying
Airless	Dusty

 Air environments

Lots of light and open air	Zen
Great views	Immaculate
Conceptual designs	Modern
Clean lines	Austere
White walls	Sterile
Balconies	Untouchable
High ceilings	Drafty
Simplicity	

 Water environments

Ancestral honoring	Open design
Water nearby	Bathtubs
Water features	Sloppy
Soft and flowy fabrics	Muddy
Curves	Corroding
Blues and greens	Leaky
Indoor-outdoor	Moldy

At Home with the Elements: Practice

Once you have completed the inventories, discuss with a friend, write about, or make an art piece around what you discovered.

Beyond the Physical

Everyone's living space has a *feel* to it. If we don't intentionally consider this, we may not notice it, but we—and others who spend time in that space—will feel it. Whether we know it or not, the minute someone walks into our living space, they get a strong feeling of its emotional temperature. The more conscious we can become about the feelings we want to cultivate in our shelters, the more effective we will be in creating the emotional environment we want.

What feelings do you want to host in *your* home? Try these two assessments.

Assessment: The Feeling of Your Home

From the following lists, pick four key feeling states that you want yourself and others to experience in your living space. Talk with someone close to you about why these feeling states are important to you, and how you intend to cultivate them more consciously on a daily basis.

Fire

☐ Dynamic   ☐ Engaged

☐ Exciting   ☐ Affectionate

☐ Creative   ☐ Expressive

☐ Passionate

◉ Earth

☐ Warm
☐ Connected
☐ Tactile
☐ Holding
☐ Hugging
☐ Dependable

☐ Consistent
☐ Ritualistic
☐ Routine
☐ Emotional and
   nurturing

◉ Air

☐ Breezy
☐ Conversational
☐ Busy
☐ Talkative
☐ Informative
☐ Inclusive

☐ Inviting
☐ Open-minded
☐ Interested
☐ Lighthearted
☐ Variety seeking

◉ Water

☐ Considerate
☐ Helpful
☐ Dear
☐ Feeling
☐ Caring
☐ Attentive

☐ Containing
☐ Empathetic
☐ Understanding
☐ Merging
☐ Boundaryless

Now go back through the lists and pick the four *least* important nurturing states in your home. The qualities you selected as

least important can be areas to grow in and bring more into your environments.

The feelings we tend to sideline as least important have a habit of coming through the back door in less invited ways. For example, if I circle "conversational" as a least-valued state, I might allow screen time constantly or have rigid rules about when people may speak or address certain topics. The things we prioritize naturally get our best attention, and the states we ignore become unsavory attention-getters.

Shadow Elements

Shadow emotions are those we tend to bury because they are not socially liked or appreciated. Anger, fear, grief, frustration, and sadness are a few examples. To the degree we do not recognize that each element has a feeling shadow, we throw off these shadow vibes without knowing it:

Fire: Caustic, impatient, battling, argumentative, righteous, loud

Earth: Suffocating, stubborn, judgmental, picky, inflexible

Air: Preoccupied, disassociated, cold, scattered, aimless, spiritually bypassing (refusing to acknowledge shadow issues; going around or over them, straight into positivity)

Water: Highly sensitive, thin-skinned, subjective, moody, secretive, contemptuous

Don't be afraid to notice the shadow feelings that exist in your home. Once you become more intentional and aware of the emotional qualities that you have neglected, or that you have not seen as important in the home, you can begin to honor them more thoroughly. Because my partner is strong in water and I am strong in air, we cultivate a caring and open feeling environment. Sometimes, the shadow sides of water or air come through: I can be cold, ending conversations and parties abruptly; and my partner sometimes brings a moody vibe because of her profound sensitivity. We are both learning how to manage these parts of ourselves in ways that protect others from being hurt.

In my case, when I am about to kick people out of my house because I am *done* with socializing and because it's past 9:00 P.M. and that's my bedtime, I'll often go to good-spirited, self-deprecating humor: "Okay! I am about to be the ice queen and kick you all out, because I'm exhausted," and then reassurance that *it truly isn't them, it's me*: ". . . but I want you to know how much I love you and that I am glad you came." I know I have this shadow side—it's just part of my makeup with so much air and fire—and so I don't judge myself or think I should pretend to be ready to party into the night when I've absolutely had it and want to go to bed. Before I understood this, I would pretend because I thought it would make me more liked and loved. The shadow ended up building a head of steam that would blow out in unconscious ways ultimately far more harmful than my telling the truth in the moment.

Self-awareness is key to mitigating the negative effects of shadow feelings. You can't find the light if you do not see the contrasting darkness.

Shadow Elements: Practice

Consider—in a conversation, journaling, or through making art—how you might work with your shadow sides the way I described my partner and me working with ours.

Refining Your Environment

How close are you to living in the environment that pleases you most? What little things can you do to add more elements to your current space that support your well-being?

Of course, if you are sharing a home with others, as most of us do, you will need to compromise with them about the elemental expressions in the spaces you share. Once you recognize what is missing from the home for you in terms of elemental balance, you can talk with those who live with you about what they most want and need. Having them complete the assessments can help facilitate this conversation. Here are a few stories about folks who worked with elements to enhance their home spaces.

When I first visited Paul and Jan, they lived in a very cave-like house—not surprising, as they were both born under the fixed earth sign of Taurus. This house represented the cozy, calm, warm, welcoming aspects of their souls. Entering it, I felt a constant invitation to be cuddled and nourished. Over time, Paul and Jan decided that they wanted to build a home that truly reflected their artistic and visionary natures. They hired dear friends and artists to create a custom home that still felt earthy and grounded, but that integrated high ceilings, mystical art, a huge fireplace, and a water feature. A more equal balance of the elements transports visitors to otherworldly dimensions while still providing beautiful safety and holding.

My teen godson Noah's bedroom reflects his Taurus Moon (dark, cave-like, cozy) and his Gemini Sun and Libra rising (movie projector and a large screen for watching the anime shows he loves). It has cool colors (grays and greens) and lots of meaningful objects scattered on every surface. As he passes from boyhood to manhood, Noah struggles with feeling motivated to achieve in school and to engage himself in a career path. I've advised him to add some fire elements to his room—a vivid red blanket for his bed and some artwork with reds, yellows, and oranges on the wall—and he reports back that this has helped him feel like he wants to lean into things with a bit more energy.

We call my friend Marla's place the Mermaid House. Every wall in this beach home honors sea creatures and nymphs; the home oozes magic and playfulness. It has a delicious combination of drama and color and an expansive softness and tenderness throughout. When you enter this house, you feel both whimsical and safe. This home is the ultimate combination of fiery, creative expression and watery, all-embracing love.

Gerardo and Shiva, both pioneering creatives in the tech and art worlds, are creating their opus home—the ultimate air and earth house. Sweeping curves and views lift the visitor to the heights of imagination. Inside this home, one feels the spaciousness of the divine coupled with the unlimited reach of the intellect.

Jayce and Shelly have dedicated their lives to building homes as works of art. They are investing considerable time, energy, and money toward developing an ecologically sustainable model of a working ranch and multiple-family compound. Their ranch is built from repurposed barns, run by solar panels, and nourished by recycled water sources. High ceilings inside and hiking trails all over the property bring a sense of spaciousness and inspiration. When I enter their ranch, I feel all the elements dancing together: the joy and happiness of fire; the steady, stable glory of earth; the exhilaration of air; and the maternal flow of water.

Emotional Intelligence

Where we feel safe to explore and express our emotional selves, we will feel most at home. The ability to do this isn't something we're born with, and it isn't something most of us learned while we were growing up. What many of us learned is to mask, hide, or disguise our emotional selves. As we develop the ability to identify, feel, and express emotions in healthy ways, we develop emotional intelligence. The more emotionally intelligent we become, the more we can feel at home wherever we go. If we are resistant to our feeling selves, nowhere will truly feel like home to us.

As children, most of us learned to mask uncomfortable emotions like fear, anger, frustration, shame, or grief to try to fit in or keep important people close. You can begin to get more comfortable with all kinds of emotions by exploring your feeling self through each of the four elements. When you recognize a strong emotion, take some time to consider the following: How do you actually feel, emotionally (water element)? How is that feeling coming through your sensations and senses (earth element)? How do you name what you feel (air element)? And, how do you express those feelings (fire element)? Exploring our feelings through the four elements is a way both to honor their power and wisdom and to reduce their ability to overwhelm us or trigger us to make choices that contradict our values. This is the first step toward feeling truly at home in yourself.

The skill of naming feelings deserves a closer examination. It involves *emotional granularity,* where we build our aptitude for accurately labeling what we feel. Naming a feeling state takes us a long way to the ability to manage it: simply naming it tames it. Where we don't name our feelings, we are often "run" by them— and they can drive us to act out in unskillful ways that don't align with our values.

Although at times, strong emotions can make us feel like we're underwater or suffocating, or like we are being completely blown away or burned to the core, they also provide us with vital messages about our innermost needs and wants. Most of us have been taught to set aside what we feel in order to get things done, but we cannot sequester, censor, or repress feelings and have wholesome, happy lives. On the other hand, it isn't healthy to dwell in the world of feelings to the point that nothing gets done. Expertise around emotions means having methods and strategies to fully feel and deal with them without them pulling us underwater. Developing this expertise enables us to host feelings as part of our everyday repertoire without letting them take over.

ILLUMINATIONS

People with fire or water signs on the fourth-house cusp, like Aries or Scorpio, might find it harder to resist acting out feelings. Fire signs like Aries, Leo, and Sagittarius may tend to act out rage or frustration with yelling, throwing things, or slamming doors; and water signs like Scorpio, Cancer, and Pisces might lean toward dramatic expressions of big feelings, playing the victim and trying to draw others in to rescue them.

Each of the elements brings something important to the big picture of building emotional intelligence:

Fire: cultivates the ability to manage intense emotions and express them skillfully instead of acting them out unskillfully.

Earth: cultivates the ability to delay gratification so you can work toward a long-term goal or effort with patience and resolve.

Air: cultivates the ability to name and tame your emotions and to reset to a positive narrative and frame of mind when you are challenged with adversity or obstacles.

Water: cultivates the ability to feel your feelings and attune
to others with compassion and empathy.

Let's say Waylon likes to keep the house clean and tidy, and
his partner, Melanie, and their teen children tend to be on the
messy side. Waylon comes home once again to a messy kitchen
with coffee-ground-strewn countertops and a sink full of dirty
dishes. He feels angry and frustrated, and rather than naming
those feelings, he might noisily and passive-aggressively clean
up and make snide, sarcastic comments to anyone who comes
through. This causes others to become angry and frustrated and
makes a real conversation about everyone's needs and responsibilities impossible. Melanie notices he's pissed off and asks him
what's up, and he says, "Oh, *nothing,* I'm *fine,* don't worry about
me," and she, feeling rebuffed, retreats. Waylon might even ac-
cidentally break a dish in his fit of pique. He's being run by his
feelings. He has lots of water and fire in his chart, and his way of
unskillfully responding to anger and frustration involves feeling
sorry for himself and as though he's being victimized (water),
and acting out (fire).

Now, let's say Waylon decides to apply the skill of emotional
granularity and naming it to tame it. This skill set incorporates
earth (delaying the gratification he might get from being snitty
or exploding at the people he's annoyed with in order to work
toward the longer-term goal of having others lend more support
with the housework) and air (communicating about feelings
rather than acting them out and resetting to a more positive
frame of mind). He might call Melanie and the teens into the

kitchen to say, "When I come home to a messy kitchen after a long day of work, I feel angry and frustrated. I feel hurt that others in this house, who know that having things tidy really matters to me, aren't doing their part to keep it nice. I need you to come in here and clean this up while I go have my shower. Can you finish this in the next half hour?" The others can negotiate this with him and then (hopefully) will do their part.

Another example: Sarah and her partner recently broke up and Sarah is grieving and sad. Her chart has plenty of earth and air, and her way of dealing with her emotions is to go deep into a depressive state: she stays home and doesn't talk to people about how she's feeling (unskillful earth), while going around and around in mental circles about how awful her situation is and how she did everything wrong and will never find another person to love (unskillful air). What will most help Sarah is to call upon the elements of water and fire: to feel her sadness and grief fully and reach out to others with the kind of compassion and empathy she most needs for herself (water) and to work on ways to skillfully express and release her deep feelings—perhaps through creative work or intense physical activity (fire).

Onward . . .

Where we live and how we feel there have a powerful impact on our daily lives, including how nourished we feel in our private time and how others feel cared for in our homes. We can live into our best expressions of ourselves by balancing the elements in both the look and feel of the homes we create.

Cultivating emotional intelligence helps us and our loved ones feel more at home no matter where we are. Each element can be drawn upon to support emotional intelligence in a different way. Where an element is less represented in our natal charts, we can make a more concerted effort to cultivate it in our journey toward greater emotional intelligence.

CHAPTER FIVE

The Fifth Domain: Creating and Loving

The two most important features of the fifth astrological house are how we create and how we fall in love. These features are the focus in our exploration of the fifth domain.

Creativity and love actually have a lot in common. To freely create, we need to step into the unknown; and anyone who has ever fallen head over heels in love knows that is the biggest leap into the unknown any of us will make.

Many of my clients complain about feeling stuck in their creative expression. It's no wonder, as social media and pop culture have many of us convinced that we shouldn't bother with creative expression unless it helps us attain fame or wealth. A casual scroll through one's social media feed is likely to pull up multiple examples of highly accomplished entertainers and artists doing their thing, and it's a natural human tendency to compare ourselves with those who draw the most views and likes. We feel we have to be good enough at our chosen form of expression to be recognized or acclaimed, or we probably shouldn't bother.

When I hear people say, "I am not very creative"—which I hear people say far more often than I would like—the unspoken message I hear is "I am almost dead." The word *create* means "to bring into being." When we forget that the most magical thing about being human is that we can consciously bring things into being, we have lost our divine spark.

The way back is through the fifth domain, which is about childlike curiosity, play, and love. Little children don't create from goals or deadlines, or subject to approval, and their creations are free and come from love. That's the kind of expression we are invited into by the fifth domain: the kind that taps into our unlimited source without censorship, expectation, or judgment. The good news is that all of us were probably fully expressive children at some point—full of wonder and amazement and ready at any moment to freely express. We can all regain that part of ourselves if we decide that it's important to us, and if we commit to a consistent creative practice.

Although the ingredients for maintaining a creative practice are simple, they do require commitment:

1. Figure out your access routes to the creative. It has been proven that we are more likely to do creative things that are within reach. For example, have coloring pens and papers on

the kitchen table, or put the guitar you want to play right next to the living room couch.

2. Gather an accountability partner or group that you can play with or share your work with.

3. Pick regular times when you will play with your creative side *no matter what,* whether it's five minutes a day drawing with your kids; an hour once a week making clay sculptures with your besties; thirty minutes on Tuesdays and Saturdays writing poems or doing collage with your partner; three hours a week learning to play a musical instrument; or any other form of creative expression you choose. The important part is making the time spent in creativity *regular* and *sacred.*

The elements that are strongest for you bring both gifts and challenges to the realm of creative expression. Drawing on the elements less fully expressed for you can help you move through resistance and realize your unique expressive potential, and the best way to bring in those weaker elements is through joining with others who naturally have elemental strengths you lack.

A few examples: my good friend Silvia has so many genius ideas that she could lift right off into space if it weren't for the grounding influence of earth companions. My dreamy friend Cat has so many devotional and empathetic feelings about her creative expressions that sometimes she needs hard earth realities to push her out of just imagining and feeling and into action. My totally earth friend Alina can get completely bogged down in details and functions; she needs a bunch of fire play to engage her creative brilliance more joyfully. A fire-type creative—which is what I am—can start a bonfire of creativity without blinking; but I need my earth friends to help me stay the course and complete the projects I start, and I need my water partners to help me remember that the ignition of my ideas can sometimes burn others.

✦

ILLUMINATIONS

Do you know what astrological sign sits on the cusp of your fifth house? If you do, these tips can help you start your creative flow:

Aries: Go big or go home. Leap into your process. Find great allies to do the editing and organizing.

Taurus: Start with your hands. Make something just for the pleasure of molding the idea.

Gemini: Speed-write or rant and record it. Use dictation if you can't sit still. Be willing to ramble and amble at first in any discipline.

Cancer: Cook up your creative side. Brew things with others. Reward all efforts with delicious meals.

Leo: Playact. Make believe. Wear costumes to get in the mood. Enroll others in the fantasies and role plays of your imaginative ideas.

Virgo: Make *doing it* the priority instead of getting it right. Never be the one to judge your creative work. Focus on volume of work rather than perfect output.

Libra: Draw, paint, or dance every day. Your creativity is your source of spiritual joy.

Scorpio: Consider making ugly and trashy an art form. The dark side is your jam.

Sagittarius: Run a mile, then sit down to create. For you, freedom in creativity is like traveling the world. When you want to flee to other places, be willing to travel inside your imagination instead.

Capricorn: Make creativity an accomplishment in and of itself. If you discipline yourself to creatively express without a specific reason, you will find a gateway to relaxation.

Aquarius: For you, friendship is a creative process. Regularly gather friends for creative projects and events.

Pisces: Your dream life holds endless suggestions for fulfilling self-expression. Keep track of your dreams and create from them in any medium.

Assessment: Qualities of Creativity

Look over this list of qualities that can show up in creative expression. Then:

1. Underline the ways you access your creative side.
2. Circle the ways you *wish* you could access your creative side, and identify folks in your life who have that gift. (You can partner with those people on their creative journeys and learn

from them; or you can just learn how to channel their flavor of creativity when you need more of what they've got.)

3. Cross off your unskillful points of creative access and recognize the cues that lead to those expressions. (For example, when, as a fiery type, I take on too much, I get to the place where I just want to *burn it down* because I am so burnt out. I know I am approaching that fiery ridge when I start to pile up resentments toward my co-creatives, and I've learned to take those resentments as a cue that I need to step back.)

 Fire

Impassioned	Impatient
Fired up	Exhausted
Energized	Impulsive
Decisive	

 Earth

Grounded	Stuck
Anchored	Stubborn
Directed	Withholding
Patient	

 Air

Inspired	Scattered
Spirited	Suffocated
Clear	Distracted
Visionary	

Water

Immersed	Drained
Connected	Lost
Flowing	Murky
Responsive	

Qualities of Creativity: Practice

If you want more fun and joy, commit to being creative every day for no reason other than that it gives you access to your positive, childlike nature. Five minutes a day of free, playful creativity, no matter what element you focus on, will increase your happiness quotient. Why not start now?

Love and Romance Through the Elements

The fifth domain is the source of juicy aliveness. Creativity and love are the keys to a life filled with joy. Anyone can create and anyone can love. We cannot wait for these spigots to be turned on from the outside. If you want more energy and vitality, start a creative practice. If you want love in your life, be more loving and affectionate with others.

This domain is also about romantic love. A look at romance through the lens of the elements helps us understand its natural stages. These stages don't necessarily progress in this order, but every lasting love will move through them all.

STAGE ONE: FIRE

Longing and Lust

It always starts with a spark: a look, a gesture, a word, a scent. Seemingly out of the blue, some human being moves from ordinary mortal to god or goddess in your eyes. It's as though an enormous, luminous aura suddenly surrounds them. Where you once saw muted colors, everything around this person becomes a vibrant panorama of buoyant, bold brilliance.

In this phase, your world feels turned on its axis. You feel a fresh surge of motivation and inspiration. You might even feel drugged by the neurochemical stew your brain is creating in response to the object of your affections. Newly turned on and perpetually excited, you've leapt from certainty and stability into rapturous unknowing. You cannot wait to see this person; you cannot wait to hear their voice. Everything starts mobilizing and organizing around contact with this love object.

STAGE TWO: EARTH

Doing Everything to Look Good to the Other

This stage is where you move out of fantasy and into a true experience of love and romance. It's still in the very beginning phase of newness and innocence, before you know whether the feelings are mutual—maybe starting with flirting and flattery, winks or turns of the head, or extraordinarily coincidental meetings or reasons to talk. You start dressing for the beloved, feeling like a mortal who wants to bejewel yourself for divine meetings with this god or goddess who has captured and enraptured you.

In this stage, people want to look and feel their best. Elevated by your contact with this luminary figure, you feel as though you could do *anything*. You can get up and exercise like you never have before; you can be witty and intelligent in conversation; you can suddenly cook like a gourmet chef. This new love powers a battery of interest that fuels your days. As flirting and flattering and giving thoughtful little gifts lead to saying how you feel, and when that feeling is reciprocated, well . . . things really tend to speed up.

STAGE THREE: WATER

Sharing Deep, Passionate Contact and Feeling

Now we move into full-on idealized love. An amazing feeling of rightness, luck, and abundance coincides with fantasies about what this connection could be and could mean. Usually, in this stage, there's the consummation of the sexual union, and all the possibilities for bell-ringing, glorious sensual and soulful physical congress are realized. (Even if the physical act is not so great, when all other factors are in place, it feels like it was all meant to be.) Your focus falls into the deepest depths of the object of your admiration. Everything seems to have led you to this place, with this person loving you and you loving them.

If you're lucky, you'll spend a generous amount of time in this stage. The more frustrated you are by how rarely you are able to see one another, the longer this period lasts. The idealized bubble continues as long as you don't get to know the mortal clay of the other person. And, over time, inevitably, there comes the next phase . . .

STAGE FOUR: AIR
Doubt and Insecurity

In this stage of romantic love, the mind is unleashed, with all its fears and insecurities. Each of you begins to see the human beneath the god or goddess that has been so entrancing and bewitching. This phase *always* brings up mental doubts and questions about you or about them. Jealous or mistrustful thoughts may creep in. At this point, people get very concerned about the future. *Where is all this going?* When anyone falls off a pedestal—which everyone does, eventually—there's disappointment.

There is nothing more intoxicating than being seen as a god or goddess or seeing someone else as a god or goddess. And when those ideals invariably fade, there's a lot of emotional hurt and disappointment. This leads into another version of the fire stage.

STAGE FIVE: RETURN TO FIRE
Battling for Power

Where there are two flesh-and-blood humans instead of gods and goddesses, not everything can be overcome with ebullient love. Conflicts arise around different needs, wants, and desires and concerns about time, money, and the sharing of responsibilities. Conflicts also arise around inevitable betrayals of the idealized images you created of each other.

In this stage, there's a lot of "You used to . . . and *now* you . . ."—as in "You used to wake up and sing to me first thing every morning . . . and now you just *grumble* at me." Or "You used to say I was the only person you wanted to touch or cuddle or make love to . . . and now you're saying you're attracted to other people?" (A side note: Anyone who says they are *never* attracted to someone besides their partner either is in the first three stages of romantic love . . . or is lying.) People begin to keep score. They start censoring themselves and damming up their feelings. The feeling zone becomes a real minefield of possible repression and (sometimes) explosion. This brings you to the next stage.

STAGE SIX: RETURN TO EARTH
Getting Real and Doing the Work

No longer blindly in love, people have to get more realistic and reflect: *What are we doing here? Who are we to each other? Who am I in this relationship? Who are you in this relationship?* This is the time to begin to examine what each of you *do* in the relationship, and what your values are. Where are your values shared, and where do they differ? What's the workaround for places where there are differences?

As you begin this stage of discernment, you realize that

phases characterized by idealization are not accurate assessments of either person. You start to look deeply into the reality of being with this human being over time. If you are skillful, you start managing your emotions better, choosing to *talk about* your feelings bravely and vulnerably rather than acting them out in hurtful ways.

If you make it past this stage, you have a more grounded idea of what's possible. You start planning for the future, which brings a more evolved version of the air stage.

STAGE SEVEN: RETURN TO AIR
Sharing Values Explicitly and Planning Futures

"Here's my idea!" "Here's *my* idea." "I hear your idea and here's how it can work with mine!" This is a time where you begin negotiating. You intentionally create reliable structures, routines, and rituals that define you as a pair or two people in love. This is where you start making more passionate emotional attachments with each other's friends and family. What was once an automatic passion takes some tending. You have to objectively decide to make intimacy a priority, and you have to plan for it.

If you get through this stage of starting a future together, you will move into the next and final stage—arguably the most soul-challenging and difficult, but one that yields incredible richness, growth, and depth of connection.

STAGE EIGHT: RETURN TO WATER

Compassion, Forgiveness, Vulnerability, and Transparency

No matter what you do, if a romantic love lasts through to this point, loss and trauma become part of the journey. There may be despair, extreme feelings of hopelessness, or just a realization that daily life, even in love, is saddled with heavy responsibilities and hardships. Sometimes it's you who has the dark night of the soul; sometimes it's your beloved. Whenever any human goes through a dark night of the soul (and every human does), the person with them feels despair, so either partner's dive to the depths is felt exquisitely by both. Alongside any losses and traumas is often a sense of "Oh, is this all there is?" rather than the bright, sparkling, flawless future you once saw on the horizon.

During this stage, one or both partners may realize that within this romantic love bond, they need some autonomy and distance to maintain a relationship with themselves. They may need to make adjustments to create this space. For partners who don't want some separation for themselves, this process can be confronting and bring up deep early wounds.

This is where real intimacy becomes possible; vulnerability becomes more needy and raw. You have to really learn to depend on each other: not in a dependent or codependent way, but in a way that makes it safe and welcome for either one of you to say to the other, "Hey, I'm really hurting and I need you right now." (Another side note: *Need* is not a four-letter word. It's a word of power and assertion.) Both partners can lean on the warmth of a shared history—where you can always draw on memories that remind you about why each of you chose the other—to sustain you through hard times.

If you can hang on through all of this, you learn that no two people can be everything to one another. No one gets through romantic love alone! True love needs reflection and responsiveness from trusted others. And so, you start to reach out to other people, and to integrate your coupling more and more deeply with your sacred crew (see Chapter 11).

When you make it through trauma and loss, past betrayals and inevitable petty resentments and feelings, you get to a place of deep, authentic emotional sharing based on trust and total vulnerability, and of resilience based on a history of surviving hard times hand in hand. You know you can count on each other and see each other through, and you have a joint commitment to truly listening to and understanding one another. You know that things thrown in your path will not take away from the deep abiding love you have worked hard to build and preserve. You keep a steady flame of passion made of equal parts respect and desire: where you no longer have that flip-of-a-switch need to jump each other's bones, but instead have an ardent desire to truly *make love* with one another.

The initial phases of romantic lust and love are always selfish. They are driven by a gargantuan need to be mirrored and to be excited. For that romantic love to truly grow and last, it has to transform. And the truth of it all is that as you move through these stages, you retain their strengths within this love relationship: passion (fire), resources and systems built together (earth), shared visions of the future and insights into the present (air), and vulnerable, caring, authentic ways of connecting (water).

True Tales of the Fifth Domain: Romantic Love

Haymi is the loveliest man you could ever meet: friendly, attractive, and successful. But he's had a really hard time with romantic love because he has a perpetual need for novelty. He's addicted to the first stages, full of unbridled, energetic lust and idealization. As soon as the lust fire becomes more like a candle, he starts to feel unmotivated and unseen. Like many people, he has bought into the myth of romantic love. If the torch isn't burning all the time, something's wrong.

Many of my clients have fallen into believing this myth. The media, in large part, has depicted romantic love as a constantly burning flame, without equal time given to depictions of all the ways in which it transforms and develops. Haymi's limited and limiting beliefs about love have tossed him, time and time again, through complete heartbreak. Venus in Aries with Jupiter conjoined in Haymi's chart emphasize a tendency toward grandiose and impulsive love. The flames never lick his heels long enough. He cannot tolerate seeing an ordinary person in his beloved, and he cannot tolerate being seen as an ordinary person *by* his beloved. Always, at a certain point in the relationship, he feels empty and bereft, and he believes that this means it's time for him to move on.

Someone like Haymi has to learn to bring things down to earth. Most people with a fire addiction—those who want things to always be hot—have trouble with their own clay feet. They are unwilling to see themselves or others as mortal, and they want to live in an idealized place. Usually this has to do with a desire to ward off feelings of emptiness and depression, which are impossible to feel when in the early, fiery flush of new love. My work with him has focused on helping him to see and appreciate the exquisite romance of everyday life, and to recognize that not all passion is defined by irresistible attraction. In order for Haymi to really integrate this understanding, however, he will have to face his own emptiness and depression. He will have to accept that he is fundamentally self-medicating with the potent neurochemicals of early-stage romantic love, and he will have to know that he can go without them in order to construct a truly lasting intimate partnership.

Jane is really good at the earthy part of romantic love as she has her Sun, Moon, and rising in earth signs. She is extraordinary at building rituals and routines, at feeding and caretaking. She thrives in an atmosphere of transactional gifts and chores that demonstrate love, care, and affection. Where she's really lacking is in the element of fire. When we dug into this in our sessions, she discovered that her reluctance to experience her own fire had to do with shame and fear: the way she experiences lust doesn't fit the mainstream model of domesticity, and it features some forbidden desires. She is also afraid that if she allows her fire to light up, she will revert to some of the risky sexual activities she engaged in when young.

Jane needs to talk vulnerably and candidly with her partner

about her lack of fire. What kinds of activities can they do together that would be both dangerous and safe, both adventurous and secure? How can they investigate together what is missing and consider ways to build a flame that doesn't destroy?

Raquel's issue is that she's all in her head: too much air. She's constantly thinking about romantic love, wondering about romantic love, and having neurotic doubts about romantic love, but she won't actually come down to earth or fire—to her, that would mean getting burned or suffocated, which happen to be her two biggest fears. She stays in the clouds with her Mercury and Mars in the sign of Gemini: analyzing everything from afar, looking at how it doesn't add up to be with this person or that person, and deeply missing out on the human experience of falling in love.

Let's consider what this phrase "falling in love" means. In order to surrender to another person in the way we do when we're madly in love, we have to allow the ego, the controlling one, to be decentered. We have to let ourselves be hurled into the unknown. We have to be willing to be hurt. We intentionally let go of the part of us that is most grounding and allow ourselves to be thrown into circumstances where we can't predict the outcome, and where a great deal is at stake.

Raquel and I talked about what this meant for her. She came to see that in order to trust enough to surrender and fall in love, she had to do some deep inner child work. A very young part of her believed that if she were to go ahead and fall for someone, she might crash and die. Beyond this, she could come to trust that sure, she might get bruised if she took that chance, but she would also gain access to an incredible, full, elemental experience of love.

Marci drowns in the element of water when she starts dating people. She has a Cancer Moon and a Pisces rising, and her Sun in Virgo is squared by the dreamy planet Neptune. She goes right to helpless, hopeless romantic feelings. The objectivity of air is missing; so is the rigor of earth and the passion of fire. She just can't extricate herself from the water faucets of emotion. The minute she starts dating somebody, she goes into a primal, needy place of "Do you love me? Will you love me? Do you care about me at all?" Not surprisingly, this is a buzzkill for her and for her prospective partner. Without the thrill of the fire, the daily earthly routines of romantic love, or the ability to look clearly at what is going on, her relationships never seem to get off the ground.

What Marci needs is deep emotional management work through a kind of therapy called cognitive behavioral therapy. Through this perspective, she'll learn that feelings are not prophecies, and that being a deep feeler is not situation-specific for her. She feels deeply about everything, and not all of these feelings should be foisted upon prospective partners. Journaling and conversations with trusted friends will help her slow down and move through a more natural and balanced process of sussing out romantic possibilities.

Assessment: Love Through the Stages

1. Circle the stages of love you most identify with, or in which you have spent the most time in your romantic life.

2. Then put check marks next to the stages you identify with least or have spent the least time in.

3. If you are in a romantic relationship, draw an X next to the stage you think you are in right now.

☐ Fire, first round: longing and lust

☐ Earth, first round: doing everything to look good to the other

☐ Water, first round: sharing deep, passionate contact and feeling

☐ Air, first round: doubt and insecurity

☐ Fire, second round: battling for power

☐ Earth, second round: getting real and doing the work

☐ Air, second round: sharing values explicitly and planning a future

☐ Water, second round: compassion, forgiveness, vulnerability, and transparency

Romance and Love Through the Elements: Practice

Consider your responses to the assessment. Spend some time writing, talking with someone close to you, or making art about your biggest takeaways.

What invitations do you sense in what you have learned? Where are you already strong and insightful about what's required for your love to last (or for you to find new love if you are not in a romantic partnership right now)? What elements could you stand to fortify, and which might be running the show in a way that doesn't promote the partnership you want?

Onward . . .

No matter where you are in terms of romance, you can bring more fifth-element love into your world. Start writing loving and expressive emails, letters, or texts to folks you care for. Bring in all the elements: allow yourself to be spontaneously loving in your everyday life (fire); do concrete acts of loving service (earth); share positive ideas and inspiring stories (air); and make a point of being vulnerable and caring, allowing space for feelings (water). Every time you think, act, plan, make something, or feel from a space of creativity and love, you feed a field that serves the good of all.

The Sixth Domain: Habits of Health

The sixth domain is all about habits and practices. To have stellar mental health and physical well-being, we need to have both helpful habits and consistent practices that upgrade our energy systems and our attitudes. We all have some good habits; we also all have unhelpful habits. Practices can be hard to maintain over time. Success in the sixth domain means building on good habits to such a degree that the unhelpful ones are mitigated, and committing to practices that are manageable while leaning on members of our sacred crew (see Chapter 11) as accountability helpers.

The world we're in makes it hard to devote the time and energy to self-care practices that most of us need to feel our best. Every day is a chance to start again (fire), keep our word about what we say we will do to increase our health (earth), re-inspire ourselves (air), and forgive ourselves for our past mistakes and find emotional support that will help us maintain habits (water). Reminder: You are human.

Health habits are no place for perfectionism. You will never be in *perfect* health; aim for the best health you can be in today. Know that self-care is community care. You can only truly replenish others when you are full.

ILLUMINATIONS

The sixth astrological house is ruled by the sign of Virgo. Virgo reflects the aphorism "God is in the details." The sixth house is never about making big promises or sweeping generalizations when it comes to our health. It is more about the nitty-gritty daily attention we give to—and small acts we perform for—our proverbial temple.

Here are tips for the sign in the sixth house to get healthy habits going:

Aries: Make sure to start each day with a fired-up exercise routine, even if it's only ten minutes long.

Taurus: Movement is key to your well-being. If you move enough, you can eat what you love. Stagnation is the enemy of health.

Gemini: Stop talking about your health. Get a friend who keeps you accountable on a daily basis for your health habit goals. You will do better if you have a workout/healthy eating buddy.

Cancer: Make a commitment to eating clean, real food. Pay special attention to what you drink. Consume little to no sugar.

Leo: Put some drama into your workouts. Find a playful way to exercise and enroll others to join you.

Virgo: Start each day with a reliable, predictable spiritual practice. Notice how your day always goes better when you start with this routine.

Libra: Always start your morning with beauty and balance. The key to your well-being is a temperate schedule. Overworking or not sleeping will haunt you.

Scorpio: Focus on eliminating toxic feelings and environmental pollution. Drink water every hour. Every time you pee, imagine negativity flowing out of your body.

Sagittarius: Long walks and great conversation will be your mainstays. Take daily walking adventures where you stretch your legs and your mind.

Capricorn: Climbing is your metaphor, but you need good knees to keep going. Do less, but do it with regularity.

Aquarius: Use your objective mind to set goals for your health habits; then get together to fulfill those goals with groups of people you love.

Pisces: Start each day with visualization or guided imagination of an ideal health day.

Make a short checklist of habits you will employ each day. At night before sleep, check off the ones you completed.

Assessment: Healthy and Unhealthy Habits

Our overall health is determined by small and consistent attempts to elevate all our mind and body systems. When we judge ourselves for what we do or do not do, we create resistance and resentment. Acceptance is the move that allows us to consider change from an open place instead of a pointed finger. You will notice that under each element the skillful and unskillful habits may appear as opposite. That's a good reminder that sometimes it just takes a flip of attitude and behavior to go in a better direction. Circle or check those you engage in with regularity. Notice how you feel as you consider each habit.

 Fire

- ☐ Teeth grinding
- ☐ Nail biting
- ☐ Picking at your fingers
- ☐ Picking at your face
- ☐ Scratching or itching incessantly
- ☐ Cardio exercise
- ☐ Expressive movement
- ☐ Playful outdoor activity
- ☐ Driving too fast
- ☐ Breaking things out of carelessness
- ☐ Yelling and stomping
- ☐ Punching things
- ☐ Spontaneous thoughtful gestures
- ☐ Courageous acts of protecting others from danger

☐ Daredevil feats

☐ Impulsive and excessive partying

☐ Sarcastic humor

☐ Staring at yourself in the mirror

Earth

☐ Staying up too late

☐ Sleeping in

☐ Putting on sunscreen

☐ Going out in the sun without protection

☐ Staying indoors and vegetating

☐ Eating lots of dark and leafy greens

☐ Only eating simple carbohydrates (foods made mostly
    from flour and sugar)

☐ Enjoying a lovely treat

☐ Bingeing on sugar regularly

☐ Making healthy and nutritious meals

☐ Eating fast food on the run

☐ Being on time

☐ Being late

☐ Brushing and flossing your teeth

☐ Doing laundry

☐ Wearing dirty clothes

☐ Mindfully cleaning up after yourself

☐ Leaving your messes for other people to clean up

Air

- [ ] Speaking with clarity and purpose
- [ ] Interrupting others and rambling on
- [ ] Reading inspirational and uplifting materials
- [ ] Obsessively reading bad news
- [ ] Watching elevating entertainment
- [ ] Watching crap TV in bed
- [ ] Listening to great podcasts
- [ ] Listening to music at ear-injuring volume
- [ ] Practicing a musical instrument
- [ ] Journal writing
- [ ] Reading to improve your memory and your mind
- [x] Reading schlock for distraction only
- [ ] Taking quiet time for reflection and integration
- [ ] Staying manically busy
- [ ] Speaking up
- [ ] Withholding your point of view
- [ ] Tripping often because your head is in the air
- [ ] Smoking
- [ ] Learning new things often
- [ ] Refusing to learn things
- [ ] Keeping your word
- [ ] Breaking your word
- [ ] Writing thank-you notes
- [ ] Forgetting to acknowledge gifts people have given you
- [ ] Calling people back promptly
- [ ] Ghosting people

☐ Reading and responding to emails

☐ Falling into "scroll-holes" on social media

Water

☐ Drinking water regularly

☐ Not drinking enough water

☐ Overcaffeinating

☐ Drinking too much alcohol

☐ Uplifting people with appreciation and praise

☐ Nastily gossiping about people behind their backs

☐ Asking others how you can help

☐ Mooching off people without helping out

☐ Yielding to other drivers

☐ Tailgating and cutting off other drivers

☐ Paying attention when others are speaking and making sure each person is heard

☐ Oversharing without any concern for who is not being heard

☐ Acknowledging your feelings

☐ Denying your feelings

☐ Using substances sacramentally

☐ Using substances to escape responsibility

☐ Working toward forgiveness

☐ Hanging on to blame and resentment

Healthy and Unhealthy Habits: Practice

Consider what you marked on the assessment. In what element did you mark the most? What element can you draw from to create better balance? Don't fret about unhealthy habits too much; focus on your strengths instead. Positive psychology has shown that when we use our strengths more consciously we can uplift some of our weaknesses. For example, the more time I spend meditating and exercising, the less sugar I want to eat.

Spend time discussing, journaling, or making art around the feelings that came up for you as you acknowledged the habits you already have. Don't plan for change yet, or scold yourself for unhealthy habits. Avoid jumping to resolutions to overhaul your lifestyle so you can be a paragon of green-juice-fueled health. Do, however, let yourself feel proud and celebratory around your current habits that are healthy and helpful. Remember that leaning into healthier habits is the key to making the less healthy habits less inviting.

Once you feel clear about your current habits and their impact, go through the following list of ways to increase health. Choose a few new habits to create better balance: pick one thing from each element list that you aren't already doing consistently and commit to doing it for thirty days with a chosen health partner or friend.

ILLUMINATIONS

Knowing the balance of elements in your birth chart can help you to choose the best possible habits and practices for better self-care:

+ If your chart has lots of planets in water signs, focus on kicking up the energy with fire habits.

+ If you have many planets in active, impulsive fire signs, consider slower earth habits to balance your regime.

+ If your chart is endowed with much earth energy, elevate your mind with more air habits.

+ If you have a preponderance of planets in heady air signs, anchor in some grounding earth practices and soften with some water habits.

 Fire

Regular cardio exercise

Walking adventures

Action-oriented creative expressions like singing, dancing, comedy, or improv

Group sports

Martial arts

Anything that makes you belly-laugh

 Earth

Yoga

Qigong

Massage

Eating vegetables at every meal

Gardening

Spending time in nature

A complete hygiene/grooming ritual

A complete skin care ritual

Taking care of animals

 Air

Inspirational reading

Listening to uplifting talks

Journal writing

Studying

Talk therapy

Being part of a meaningful group activity

Breath work

 Water

Taking a luxurious bath

Swimming

Daydreaming

Drinking half a gallon of water a day

Deep emotional release work

Dream journaling

Proper rest

True Tales of Transformation: Habits and Practices

Jewel has her Sun in Gemini and Venus in Aquarius in the sixth house, and she loved her vape. She used it every day to mellow out after work. But she started to feel like she could not relax without it. When she realized that vaping was her only reminder to breathe deeply and consciously, she saw that what she was really missing in her life was breath. After an online breath work class and thirty days of practice, she realized that she was less attached to her vape. She didn't quit it altogether, but she used it far less often than she once had. Jewel was happy to wake up each morning without a slight rasp in her voice, and felt less concerned about her long-term respiratory health.

At only thirty-two years old, Parker, with Taurus Sun in the sixth house and Moon and Venus in Virgo, was complaining of all sorts of aches and pains. Over the past few years, he had been moving less and less, and blamed his work schedule for keeping him sedentary. His friend Paulina, a Leo, asked him to join her for a sunrise challenge class, which would bring a small group of dedicated folks together for daily high-intensity interval training from 6:00 to 7:00 A.M. The group would also work together on shifting to healthier eating habits. It wasn't cheap, but the class leader promised a full refund after three months to anyone who was not fully satisfied. Parker went for it. After three months, he felt ten years younger—and started dating someone he met in the class.

Liz, with her Moon in Cancer in the sixth house and a highly sensitive Pisces Sun, was feeling out of spiritual alignment. She went through the motions of her life, but somehow felt like there was a big piece missing; she easily fell into rabbit holes of depression and despair. What Liz was deeply craving was a connection to a bigger source of meaning. I suggested that she learn a form of qigong that brought a sense of being lovingly embraced by the universe. Liz started practicing by herself for one week, and then joined a group of souls from all over the world to practice online twice a day. She shared with me that over time, she felt much more vitality and sense of purpose, just from adding this practice. Although her life was in theory pretty much the same, this new practice helped her feel spiritually connected and reinforced.

Tami has her Sun and Mars conjunct in Aries in the sixth house. She suffered from outbursts of anger with her partner. She would get wound up easily and then just blow a gasket. She could not find a way to stop, despite the harm her rages were causing to her relationship and to her children. I suggested to Tami that she invest in ten sessions of trauma therapy using a method called EMDR (Eye Movement Desensitization and Reprocessing) in order to get to the root causes of her short fuse. In these sessions, she delved into the hopelessness and vulnerability she'd felt as a child with a tyrannical father. She began to untangle both her hatred of that behavior and the ways in which she herself was acting it out in order to feel more powerful. She worked with her therapist to build cognitive and emotional habits and practices she can use to snuff that burning fuse before it blows.

Habits can seem small, but they make up so much of how we behave and interact. Really, each of us is more or less a collection of our strong and weak habits. We can do something about the things we want to change; no habit is unbreakable or unattainable. Whenever we're annoyed about someone else's bad habits, we can redirect our focus to getting real about the ones we have that we'd like to shift or transform. The rewards of healthy habits and practices are the energy and health we need to fulfill our dreams.

Let your natural balance of elements support you in this journey. Having lots of fire means you can start out new each day with a flame of desire for better health. Lots of earth means you are ready and able to do what you have committed to do without leaning into excuses. Abundant air means you're good at paying close attention to ideas and words that can motivate you toward great health. Plenty of water means you're a natural at connecting deeply with others around what you need, and can keep your cup filled with love and intimacy—which science is proving to be the most vital aspect of a healthy, fulfilled life.

CHAPTER SEVEN

The Seventh Domain: The Support Road Map

Being deeply loved by someone gives you strength,
while loving someone deeply gives you courage.

—LAO TZU (MOST LIKELY, HE HAD A LEO SUN WITH MOON IN PISCES)

Loneliness and social isolation pose serious risks to our health. Both are rampant in our society today, and there are solutions for both within this chapter.

The first area we'll focus on in this domain is to understand what kind of support we need, and to be explicit about it. When we know our own "support language" and take time to discover the support languages of our important people, we bypass the drama and difficulty that tend to show up when needs for support go unmet.

The second focus of this chapter is how to cultivate the qualities you most admire in others as potential untapped assets in yourself. We often long for qualities that we think others have while failing to see that we have them in ourselves and that we can choose to develop and express them. There's a saying: "You spot it, you've got it." If you can see it in others, it exists in you, and you don't have to depend on them to bring it into your relationship. Drawing from all the elements to grow those longed-for qualities in yourself will strengthen your one-to-one relationships and help you live into your fully realized self.

What's Your Support Language?

One major way in which we feel deeply connected to others is the giving and receiving of support. I've known so many people who hold a deep belief that needing others—even those who are closest to us—is a sign of weakness, and that it's burdensome to others to be leaned on. *If I were strong, capable, and smart,* they think, *I'd solve my own problems and not bother or count on anyone else to be there for me.* (These same people often long to be leaned on, because they believe that being a good person means being there for others.) Much of my work as a psychological astrologer and mentor boils down to emphasizing that everyone needs support, and that being able to ask for it from people we care about is not a sign of weakness—it's a sign of strength and wisdom, and is a key to lifelong wellness and happiness.

It isn't always clear to us or to others what true support looks or feels like. We can learn about our love languages and the love languages of others through self-help books and articles, but this doesn't quite cover the depth and breadth of the ways we can truly support one another as friends, family, work colleagues, or lovers. Once we have assembled what I call our "sacred crew" (more on this in Chapter 11), it remains our duty to learn what makes us feel most supported by them, and to develop a support language that enables us to ask for those things as part of our interdependent connection.

I've asked dozens of clients to share about how they feel most sustained by others. In talking with folks about their support language, I found that most people hadn't thought deeply about it. They certainly had not communicated those needs to their closest crew, and they did not exactly know what the members of their crew needed to feel supported by them. To help them identify their support language, I had them consider when they felt *un*supported. They shared that they feel most unsupported when others do these things:

Minimize their feelings

Talk over them or interrupt them while they are speaking

Unfairly judge or harshly criticize them

Seem checked out while they are talking

Doubt or undermine them

Compare themselves to them

Gossip about or and belittle others (because they know if they're doing it to others, they're probably doing it to them, too)

Talk behind their back

Don't let them know what they want or need from them

Don't acknowledge them

From this list, it seems clear that what people want most is to be understood and encouraged. Beyond this fundamental need, it gets more complicated. Each of us has a very specific map of what we experience as support; one size does not fit all. We might assume that if someone loves us, they'll know what we need, or we might assume that others want to be supported in the same way we do. Both these assumptions miss the mark in subtle and profound ways.

The four elements turn out to be wonderful ways to understand differing needs for support. Through examining the qualities of the four elements and recognizing yourself in them, you can start to be clearer about what your support language is and how to explain it to others. If you have a predominance of one element or another, you may see your support language reflected pretty accurately in one element category. Or you may see your support language in multiple categories. See which of these feel true for you when you want or need support.

 Fire

Support is expressed through action and bold demonstrations.

Show me instead of telling me. Bring me food, flowers, and gift certificates for experiences.

Show up when you say you will. Be someone I know will be there for me—at the time we've agreed upon.

Be truthful with me. Share your authentic feelings honestly and thoughtfully.

Celebrate me with enthusiasm and special rituals.

Acknowledge my accomplishments.

 Earth

Support is expressed through consistent effort.

Do chores—both small and big. Don't wait to be asked or count on others to cheer you on.

Give me thoughtfully selected gifts and supplies. Notice what you might give me that will best support my endeavors.

Be calm, patient, and accepting. Listen deeply and don't rush to fix me when I need to vent or work through problems.

Be dependable and consistent. I need to count on your affections and actions.

 Air

Support is expressed through communication.

Regularly speak words of affirmation and acknowledgment to me. Your words nourish and boost me up.

Be actively curious about me. Take interest in my beliefs, thoughts, and ideas, and ask me great follow-up questions.

When I am upset, please take deep breaths with me. This helps me find my center.

Be willing to disagree with me in a respectful way. Always look for what we have in common.

Water

Support is expressed through genuine feeling.

Be a safe container for me to share my deep feelings and
sensitivities. Recognize that I have big emotions that
sometimes feel overwhelming to me.

Treat my issues with empathy and compassion. Validate my
concerns.

Be present and attentive when you are with me. Make me
the priority when we are together.

Trust that I will be okay even when I am in a dark place.
Give me space.

Keep in mind that your support needs might differ in different settings and with different people. In my partnership, for example, I experience support when she gives me consistent words of encouragement and is fascinated by my creative ideas; there, my support profile falls mostly within the element of air. My partner experiences support when I do lots of chores without any nudging or need for acknowledgment—an earthy kind of support. When we both remember to prioritize these support needs, we feel buoyed and loved.

At work, my support needs are different: more earthy and fiery. I need people to be direct with me about their needs, desires, and appreciation. My Moon is in Taurus in the sixth house, so my everyday work life has to be emotionally fulfilling and very practical. My first house has Saturn and Mars in Sagittarius, which means I am often the person at work to be authoritative and strong-willed in matters of integrity and keeping agree-ments.

The key is to find out what others in our crew need, and to try our best to give it to them. This is one of the ways we love each other. It's not hard to support someone when you know what matters to them, and there is nothing more satisfying than having your support be well received.

None of us should be tasked with knowing how to support another unless that person has told us what they need. When we remove the pressure to guess or mind-read, we can have clear communication about what effective support looks like for us and for others, and we become much more effective at holding and caring for one another. Having honest and clear conversa-tions about our support languages helps us bypass the drama and difficulty that can arise when people with differing needs for support expect others to *just know what they need*, and then get grouchy or angry or lapse into victim mode when they don't have those needs met.

Your Support Language: Practice

Sit down with your close crew to examine the support needs in each element. Take time to share with each other how you most like to be supported. State your needs as clearly as you can, and get as clear about your crew's needs as you are able. Commit to doing your best to meet those needs for each other, and be open to giving and receiving reminders when you or they fall short.

Owning Your Projections

In psychology, *projection* is often defined as the practice of disowning negative qualities in ourselves while seeing them rampantly in others—and, in some cases, demonizing others for possessing those qualities. The person angrily pointing fingers at others' desires, choices, or behaviors almost always harbors those desires, or a proclivity to make those choices or engage in those same behaviors. This is a seventh-domain problem that is also an opportunity, because there is also such a thing as *positive* projection, where we project desirable or admirable qualities that we ourselves possess—and want to awaken—onto other people. Mastering the seventh domain means looking at our own positive projections and taking them back as qualities we wish to grow within ourselves.

Consider the qualities you seek out in others. What characteristics draw you in like a moth to a flame? Are they fiery qualities like audacity, magnetism, or the ability to do a ton of tasks on any given day? Are they earthy qualities like being organized, grounded, or well resourced? Are they airy qualities like abstract intelligence or inspiring visions of what's possible? Or watery qualities like psychic abilities or the capacity for deep empathy or emotional depth?

Those qualities you wish to express and embody, and that you tend to project onto others, are likely to reflect the astrological sign that sits on the cusp of your seventh house, a spot on the natal chart also known as the *descendent* (it sits opposite the *ascendant,* or rising sign, on the other side of the chart). Growing into truly mature relationships means owning those qualities for yourself rather than counting on others to carry them for you.

For example, if you have Capricorn on your seventh-house cusp, you might tend to look up to folks who exude Capricorn qualities of industry, achievement, status, and authority. You may go a long while in your life seeing those as personal strengths that you couldn't possibly possess. You might even marry someone who is a Capricorn Sun, hoping at some level that being with that person will deliver those assets to you by osmosis.

A woman I know whose seventh house was ruled by Capricorn did just that: She married her Capricorn college sweetheart because he was already the president of many organizations and was majoring in business. Flash forward twenty-five years and three gorgeous children, and she routinely complains about how cold and distant he is, how not in touch with his feeling side he is, and how crummy she feels to have never had a job. She faces the empty nest with dread. Now she gets to confront how she psychologically hired her mate to do all the heavy lifting in terms of providing, and to reckon with how she neglected her abilities to be in the world and feel useful.

Another friend, a Capricorn Sun whose seventh house was ruled by Aquarius, idealized others who she saw as unapologetically weird and effortlessly visionary. She saw herself as mostly practical and nose-to-the-grindstone, unwilling to rock the boat or disappoint anyone; she was deeply concerned with others' impressions of her, afraid to let any kind of freak flag fly or to put energy into her own unique visions of the world. At the same time, she was endlessly fascinated by quirky individualists who seemed able to happily self-express and speak the language of possibility. In midlife, she realized that she *did* have the ability to envision and dream, and that beyond the limitations of her Capricorn identity, she had some deep weirdness to express in her own right . . . and so, she began to experiment with alternative lifestyles, unconventional fashion, edgy hairstyles, and visionary projects of her own design. Although that flowering-open has been thrilling for her, she is sad to have spent so many years of her life with a bushel over that light because she thought it only belonged to others and not to her.

The gist: Whenever we unconsciously give someone else a part of ourselves to play, we end up paying a price in terms of not feeling fully expressed. When we disavow any of our inherent expressive possibilities and assign them to others, we also tend to express the shadow sides of those possibilities.

ILLUMINATIONS

Knowing the sign that sits on your descendent, you can get some direction about how these shadow sides can show up as unskillful expressions of that sign:

Sign on seventh-house cusp	Unskillful expression
Aries	You look for bold, enterprising confidence in others; then you begin to see them as bossy, immature, and reckless.
Taurus	You look for solidity, stability, and dependability in others; then you become irritated as they come to seem stodgy, stubborn, and greedy.
Gemini	You look for highly verbal, curious, and versatile thinkers; then you become judgmental when they are all over the place and lack depth.
Cancer	You look for highly sensitive, maternal types who prioritize family; then you become contemptuous about their overinvolvement and family codependency.
Leo	You look for highly colorful and performing personalities full of fun; then you criticize how self-centered and childlike they are.

Sign on seventh-house cusp	Unskillful expression
Virgo	You look for people who are perfectionist and service-oriented; then you rail against how uptight and duty-bound they are.
Libra	You look for people who are fair-minded, gracious, and responsive; then you become impatient when they begin to seem indecisive and vain.
Scorpio	You are drawn to people with intensity, drive, and depth; then you feel resentful about their moodiness and hunger for power.
Sagittarius	You are drawn to people who speak up and out and like to explore new horizons; then you start to see them as know-it-alls who don't really listen to your opinions.
Capricorn	You look for people who are accomplished and have high status; then you feel emotionally abandoned and unimportant to them.
Aquarius	You look for people who are broad-minded and community oriented; then you complain that they love the world more than they love you.
Pisces	You look for dreamers, artists, or muses who are dripping with feeling; then you feel like you are carrying them on your back and it's a burden.

Owning Your Projections: Practice

Look over the list of projections in the preceding Illuminations box. No matter what is on your seventh-house cusp, pick two signs that represent what you tend to project onto others. Look carefully at the two sets of traits you tend to ask others to carry. Write down the names of folks you give these qualities to and take time to journal, talk, or make art around the costs of this projection.

For example: I would pick Cancer and Leo, because I often project my family bonding qualities and my self-centered, performative side onto others. I get critical of other people for seeming overinvolved with family; and at times, my family feels neglected and unloved because I seem to bond more easily with my friends. I tend to hold back from opportunities where I would be expected to step into the spotlight, and this can mean not taking the risk of putting myself out there for engagements that could be fulfilling.

Once you have identified where you are projecting these qualities on others, notice which elements they are. Start to think about how you might begin to consciously integrate these elements and attributes more into your one-to-one relationships. For example: Cancer is a water sign. My habit of projecting Cancerian qualities on others can help remind me to express more deep feelings about my love and commitment to family. Leo is a fire sign; when I notice myself thinking, *That opportunity to shine isn't really for me; it's for someone else,* I can remember how much I enjoy sharing my talents publicly, and I can choose to go for it!

Onward . . .

The work of the seventh domain is to understand what kind of support you need, and to be explicit about it. It's also about recognizing the qualities you most admire in others as potential untapped assets in yourself. Doing your work in both these areas sets you up to have maximum satisfaction in your one-to-one relationships.

Sustaining healthy, dynamic, and supportive relationships means staying awake to the expression of all four elements in our relationships:

Fire: Dynamic, charismatic, confident, courageous
Earth: Grounded, practical, industrious, helpful
Air: Lively, intelligent, curious, visionary
Water: Caring, kind, nurturing of feelings and dreams

Every time we allow ourselves to ask for support and willingly give support in the ways others want it, we help to eradicate loneliness and isolation in the world. And every time we choose to see and cultivate a quality we think only others can bring, we make the world more complete as we complete ourselves.

CHAPTER EIGHT

The Eighth Domain: Intimacy and Sex

Watch out! We've entered the eighth domain of experience . . . and it is *super hot* here.

The eighth house in astrology corresponds with sex, death, and shared resources. These areas have a common intensity: the longing to be alive, connected, and deeply engaged. This house is ruled by the transformative planet Pluto. Through sex, through death, and through merging our resources with those of others, we are transformed. For the purposes of this book, and within the eighth domain, we will focus on sex.

There is nothing more powerful and specific to humans than sexuality. It's astonishing that, in our animal bodies, we can experience such extreme pleasures with others and with ourselves; but what is most spectacular is that, unlike animals, we can experience these sensations and be conscious of them at the same time. We can simultaneously be ecstatic participants and rapturous witnesses.

ILLUMINATIONS

Mars is the old ruler of the eighth house. Some say Pluto, which was discovered in 1930, is the "big papa" of Mars. Pluto is a heavy-hitting dude who rules the underworld and the entire Earthly drama of life and death. Pluto governs transformation, death, and rebirth (think orgasm) and the spellbinding intensity of raw power and emotion. Mars reflects the instinctual nature and the primal aggressiveness that is required to initiate sexual relations.

Scorpio is the sign associated with the eighth house. The essence of this house is penetrating the deepest mysteries of life to experience immortality. Planets in your eighth house give you insight into areas of life where you will die and be reborn many times. They also can point out places where you'll have to work through toxic shame, as our culture has banished many difficult emotions to the repression zone.

For example, if you have the Moon in the eighth house, you will most likely go through intense emotional loss at times and experience profound feelings of hate, envy, or jealousy. Your tendency will be to hide those deep, dark feelings, and to want to symbolically die of shame. The ultimate healthy move for the Moon in the eighth house is to bravely find a safe person to work with—a skilled guide who can walk with you through your awful emotional bouts into a new and fresh feeling of emotional invincibility.

Our sexuality—our preferences, proclivities, and experiences, the things we've done, the things we'll *never* do, the way we feel about the things we've done and will never do, the things that turn us on and off, how private we are about ourselves as sexual beings, the ways we are sexually attracted and attract others, and the ways we think about, talk about, and reflect upon all these things—is an extraordinarily important part of our selfhood that resonates with many other parts of who we are. Taking an honest look at our sexual selves is a valuable step toward living a fully realized and extraordinary life.

Assessment: Getting It On

When you take these inventories, be as honest as you possibly can. Allow yourself to become aware of your preferences without judgment. Circle or check all that are your preferences.

Fire

☐ I like to initiate.

☐ I like to dominate.

☐ I like to be spontaneous.

☐ I like to use toys.

☐ I like to wear costumes.

☐ I like to do it vigorously.

☐ I like quickies.

☐ I like to do it adventurously.

Earth

- ☐ I like to go slowly.
- ☐ I like to linger.
- ☐ I like to be touched everywhere.
- ☐ I like a gorgeous setting for making love.
- ☐ I like to plan for it.
- ☐ I like it certain ways at certain times.
- ☐ I like lots of holding and cuddling before and after.

 Air

- ☐ I like to discuss it.
- ☐ I like sex talk.
- ☐ I get aroused by my partner's mind.
- ☐ I like to get kinky.
- ☐ I like to break rules.
- ☐ I like to make sure you get off.
- ☐ I like erotica.

Water

- ☐ I like to feel you with me.
- ☐ I like to express my feelings to you.
- ☐ I like to feel deeply connected.
- ☐ I like to look into your soul.
- ☐ I like to feel merged.
- ☐ I like to cry during or after.
- ☐ I like to feel very emotionally safe.

Touching Myself

 Fire

☐ I like to come fast and take chances about getting caught.

 Earth

☐ I like to rub oils all over my body and take my time.

 Air

☐ I like to think about it a lot before I do it and tell myself sexy things.

 Water

☐ I like to feel super safe and protected while touching myself.

Talking and Thinking About Sex

 Fire

☐ Tell me hot things . . . sometimes they can be dangerous or nasty.

 Earth

☐ Seduce me by speaking to my senses of smell, touch, taste, and sight.

Air

☐ Tell me hot stories and lure me in with clever words.

 Water

☐ Tell me how you feel about me and how close we are.

Fantasizing About Sex

 Fire

☐ I like to imagine powerful scenarios.

☐ I like to imagine dangerous scenarios.

☐ I like to imagine victory scenarios.

☐ I like to imagine highly creative scenarios.

☐ I like to imagine worship scenarios.

 Earth

☐ I like to imagine sultry sex.

☐ I like to imagine long and gorgeous seductions.

☐ I like to imagine being savored.

☐ I like to imagine intense sensuality.

☐ I like to imagine a slow and steady buildup.

 Air

☐ I like to imagine montages of union.

☐ I like to imagine equal pleasure.

☐ I like to imagine ideal bodies.

☐ I like to imagine rebellious scenarios.

☐ I like to imagine sexy conversations and spoken words.

💧 Water

☐ I like to imagine psychic sex.

☐ I like to imagine ideal intimacy and sharing.

☐ I like to imagine absolute vulnerability.

☐ I like to imagine coming as a *petite mort*.

☐ I like to imagine transformation through sex.

☐ I like to imagine dealing with jealousy through sex.

You are beginning to establish a picture of your sexual desires and needs. As we all know, sexuality doesn't exist in a vacuum. Our needs for flavors of intimacy in relationship inform how we show up in the bedroom and how we want others to show up for us. Where our intimate needs are not understood and met, it can be hard to release into full expression in this domain.

Assessment: My Intimate Needs

Circle or check all of the following statements that are true for you. If you are in a sexual relationship, have your lover take this assessment too. This is the beginning of an illuminating self-reflection, and perhaps a conversation, that could steam things up in your sex life.

Fire

- [ ] I need you to support my independence and assertiveness.
- [ ] I need you to encourage me to be physically active and strong.
- [ ] I need you to join me on brave adventures.
- [ ] I need you to support me in expressing my tender and vulnerable emotions.
- [ ] I need you to host my anger without reactivity or punishment.
- [ ] I need you to set clear boundaries regarding acceptable ways to express my anger.
- [ ] I need you to keep it new and hot.
- [ ] I need you to attract me by taking impeccable care of your body.
- [ ] I need you to take me on a whim of spontaneity and adventure.
- [ ] I need you to constantly remind me how desirable I am.
- [ ] I need you to appreciate and foster my kick-ass fire.
- [ ] I need you to value my autonomy.
- [ ] I need you to give me plenty of room to cool off before talking to me.
- [ ] I need you to emphasize my bravery and courage.
- [ ] I need you to meet my needs for passion and affection with equal energy.
- [ ] I need you to see that under my strong independence there is a need to depend on you.
- [ ] Don't try to hem me in.

☐ Don't criticize me when I am needy or tender.

☐ Don't let me focus on my needs to the exclusion of others.

☐ Don't allow me to express my anger in unhealthy ways.

☐ Don't tell me to smile.

☐ Don't tell me to be nice.

☐ Don't ask me to sit still.

☐ Don't tell me I am *too much*.

☐ Don't shame me for my desires.

☐ Don't try to get me to tone down my colors.

Earth

☐ I need your *actions*—not just the words you say—to show your love for me.

☐ I need you to be stable and consistent.

☐ I need you to hold me the way I want to be held.

☐ I need you to reassure me that how I am feeling is okay (maybe more than once).

☐ I need you to encourage me to get out of my comfort zone.

☐ I need you to support me in creating beauty and harmony.

☐ I need you to be patient with the pace of my emotional processing.

☐ I need you to appreciate my demonstrations of affection.

☐ I need you to value my need to go slowly and sensually.

☐ I need you to seduce me with sensual courting.

☐ I need you to take care to smell great.

☐ I need you to help make our environment plush and comfortable.

☐ I need you to give me poetry, flowers, foot rubs, and animal lust.

☐ I need you to encourage me to move my body in ways that are pleasure-based and joyful.

☐ I need you to be dependable, stable, and reliable.

☐ I need you to compliment me for how I give to others generously and freely.

☐ I need you to remind me as much as possible about how beautiful I am.

☐ I need you to spend lots of time with me in nature.

☐ Don't push me to do things when I need more time.

☐ Don't tell me I am *too much* for wanting physical affection.

☐ Don't make fun of the routines or rituals I use to ground myself.

☐ Don't allow me to get too hung up on material things as statements of worth or love.

☐ Don't shame me for being scared of new things.

☐ Don't take my stuff without asking.

☐ Don't let me isolate and withdraw for too long. When I do that, come and hug me.

☐ Don't let me lie around for too long watching too much TV or eating unconsciously.

Air

☐ I need time to daydream and reflect.

☐ I need lots of things to learn and talk about.

☐ I need words of affirmation and mental stimulation.

☐ I need you to talk things through with me so that I can understand you better.

☐ I need to be heard.

☐ I need humor, cleverness, and wit.

☐ I need you to regularly make time to ask me questions and listen to me deeply.

☐ I need you to encourage me to express my points of view.

☐ I need you to have direct conversations with me about what really matters to both of us.

☐ I need you to invite me into calm and focus if you see me scattered and distracted for long periods of time.

☐ I need you to be willing to learn new exciting things with me.

☐ I need you to respond to my curiosity with openness.

☐ I need you to make your requests to me simple and brief.

☐ I need you to sweet-talk me . . . and mean it.

☐ I need you to seduce me with great banter and humor.

☐ I need you to learn the words that turn me on.

☐ I need you to thrill me with variety.

☐ Don't talk over me and interrupt me.

☐ Don't tell me what I say is ridiculous or stupid.

☐ Don't overwhelm me with too much information at once.

☐ Don't tune me out while focusing on devices.

☐ Don't let me forget that I have a body too—not just a busy mind.

☐ Don't forget to laugh a lot with me.

☐ Don't ever make fun of me for crying.

💧 Water

- [ ] I need you to understand how sensitive and tender I am.
- [ ] I need you to be there for me when I am sad.
- [ ] I need you to enjoy great meals with me.
- [ ] I need you to validate how emotionally psychic I am.
- [ ] I need you to encourage me to keep my word and do what I say.
- [ ] I need you to value how much a sense of family means to me.
- [ ] I need you to help me let go of past hurts by acknowledging them.
- [ ] I need you to praise my vulnerability and transparency.
- [ ] I need you to breathe slowly and deeply with me when I get emotional.
- [ ] I need you to lovingly encourage me to take time-outs when I feel emotionally overwhelmed.
- [ ] I need you to acknowledge me when I stick to my responsibilities and commitments.
- [ ] I need you to listen nondefensively when I state my needs clearly.
- [ ] I need you to make space for truly connected time with me without others present.
- [ ] I need you to applaud my loyalty and integrity.
- [ ] I need you to seduce me by being unflappably mature.
- [ ] I need you to kiss my tears and hold me near.
- [ ] I need you to stay close with me after we make love.

☐ I need you to set limits around how much time you are
   willing to spend talking something through with me.
   (Sometimes I might not know when to stop.)

☐ Don't shame me for my neediness or tenderness.

☐ Don't take advantage of my loyalty and trust.

☐ Don't rush me through sensitive conversations.

☐ Don't allow me to hijack the day with my emotions.

☐ Don't give in to me just to get me to stop being upset.

☐ Don't retaliate when I express my valid anger.

Read through all the needs and desires you circled or checked. Consider these client stories as you begin to make use of this knowledge to grow in your eighth-domain wisdom and satisfaction. Notice how true, lasting sexual chemistry requires that lovers find ways to incorporate all elements of sexuality into their repertoire.

Don is all fire when it comes to sex. For him, the number of times he and Lauren do the deed each week has been an important measure of success in his marriage. Lauren has trouble with Don's fiery expectations and heated demands; she is mostly earth when it comes to sex. In their work with me, Don decided to do much more touching and present listening not as a means to an end but as a way of appreciating his time with Lauren; she responded with much more willingness to get hot and frisky in the moment.

Sylvia has her Moon and Venus in Libra in the eighth house. She has great shame about her sexual needs and does not feel comfortable receiving. Her biggest breakthrough in her work with me came as she began to practice exploring her needs out loud with her partner in short, protected conversations. Slowly, she began to expand her capacities for pleasure by taking on a more initiating role: she was building in herself the assertiveness of fire.

With Mars in Virgo (an earth sign) in the eighth house, Leandra was stuck in her ruts in bed; she leaned heavily on her need for routine and security. She relied on the old tried and true ways of getting off and found herself resisting sex more and more. Her earthiness was getting too heavy and weighed down with repetitiveness. She and her partner agreed that they needed to try new things, and they started watching erotic movies and reading erotica in bed. This led to them trying new moves and kick-starting their sex life.

Shaun could not get out of his head (air). He became addicted to porn images and couldn't connect to his flesh-and-blood partner. Every time he would start to have sex, his mind would be hijacked by visuals from porn. Shaun had the courage to confront this pattern, and willingly decided to quit porn for one year. At first, he felt very depressed without his self-soothing habit; but then he and his partner agreed to do slow, sensual massages once a week. This helped them to slowly reenter the power and presence of their sexual connection. Although it took Shaun about three months to get through withdrawal from his addiction, he did regain his interest in real-life sex and renewed his deep bond with his partner. He expressed enormous relief about no longer being overtaken by compulsive and distorted images and being able to return to deep intimacy in real life.

When we review all the ways we get turned on and engage

our sexual natures, we become more fully sexually expressed. When you realize that each element makes an enormous contribution to having an ecstatic sexual life, you can be more intentional about utilizing them all in ways that resonate with you. Integrating all the elements into our sex lives elevates sexual connection into the art form it has the potential to be.

The most important thing to realize is that any two people can be compatible sexually if they are willing to learn and respond to each other's sexual needs and elemental preferences. In my vast experience of astrological consultation, there is absolutely no evidence that certain sign combinations are more favorable than others in terms of coupling. It all comes down to willingness, openness, and genuine curiosity to keep the sexual spark alive.

The Elements in Your Sex Life: Practice

Decide which of these you want to bring to bed more fully:

Fire: Fast and hot
Earth: Sensual and steady
Air: Interesting and novel
Water: Steeped in feeling and depth of connection

Journal, discuss, or make art around one or two things you can do to bring that element to your love life, whether it's in your self-loving or in lovemaking with others. Let your imagination run wild; do some Internet research; talk to that one friend you might have who is naturally sexually liberated and adventurous—find a way to actualize. Then, journal, discuss, or make art about the results of your exploration, making sure to celebrate yourself for taking a chance on something new and investing time, thought, and energy in your sexual realization and satisfaction.

The Subtle Sexual Field

Lately, when I turn on movies and see the inevitable sex scene where a man picks up a woman and throws her against the wall or onto the bed without even a bit of foreplay, I wonder: *Who feels left out of this erotic portrayal?*

What about people with bad backs? Or those who don't always get turned on or stay aroused? Or the couples where one is too small to lift up the other? Or those who have histories of sexual trauma and need to be handled much more gently? Or folks who are tired and sensitive but still want to feel sexual heat and intimacy?

I am incredibly lucky to have had exquisite male and female lovers in my life and have experienced extraordinary pleasure with both. What I have learned is that athletic penetrative sex is fabulous and thrilling, but it's not always the preferred or desired move.

People who have gone through pregnancies, raising children, hormonal ebbs and flows, and debilitating illnesses can sometimes feel awful for not maintaining this acrobatic sexual prowess. Folks who are not generally looking to participate in a sexual

Olympiad can most certainly have a fulfilling sex life with variety, longevity, and space for all kinds of emotions. The key? Cultivating what I call the *subtle sexual field*.

The subtle sexual field is a place where signals, cues, and expressions are all in service of eros and sexual connection. It is created by intentionally flirting and learning the nuanced turn-ons of your partner.

When the subtle sexual field is present and engaged by both parties, the lovers feel seen, appreciated, and desired without everything aiming toward an end goal.

Here are some of the most common ingredients of a vital and ongoing subtle sexual field, grouped by element:

 Fire

Favorite foods presented in a celebratory way

Evocative clothing loved by the other

Sexy underwear

Picking out sex toys together

A naughty adventure together that may involve nudity

Dress-up fantasies and hilarious laughter

 Earth

Hair touching and sometimes brushing or combing

Head, shoulder, and foot massages

Flirty dancing

Active and frequent physical affirmations

Stroking and caressing with complete presence and no
agenda

Making the bed a silky love nest with ideal lighting and
music

Holding hands and meaning it

 Air

Inside jokes about past memorable sexual times

Romantic dates without distractions, phones, or other people

Talk about sexual fantasies that feel good to both people

Erotica read out loud to each other

Suggestive text messages

Voice messages sent, saved, and replayed

Handwritten love notes and poems

Hidden sticky notes with private erotic messages

 Water

Lingering eye contact

Deep, attentive listening

Acknowledgments of vulnerable sharing

Body painting under soft light

Some activities combine elements: sensual candles and incense are fire and earth; fragrances that evoke sultry memories
are air and earth; beautiful meals or cocktails are earth and water;
watching a sexually provocative show that is a turn-on for both
partners is fire and air; and asking the other what kind of touch
they most desire or need is air and water.

Obviously, this is not a comprehensive list, and some things
mentioned here may work for some and not others. However, if

you envision many of these things happening on a frequent basis, you'll begin to see how powerfully a subtle sexual field enriches daily life.

For most people with busy lives, the sex act itself may be brief. Living in and helping to create the subtle sexual field is a long-term adventure . . . and it's also a great habit to practice when first dating. It creates increased sexual security and confidence and reinforces an atmosphere of attractiveness and desire. Partners and lovers get more adept at knowing how to honor the erotic imagination of the other and how to prioritize sexuality in general. This also provides more opportunities for those hyperphysical acrobatics if and when they are desired.

> **If you're too busy for sex, you're too busy.**
>
> *—Esther Perel, (her Sun is in Leo and she is full of heart)*

Why do some people avoid doing these things when they can be mutually enjoyable and enhancing? Most folks want sexuality to be instant and automatic, as it tends to be in the first months with a new partner. They want to feel that uncontrollable urge to do anything and everything to get with this delicious new person in their lives.

Once the chemical cocktail of novelty wears off, somewhere between six months and two years of being together, whipping up desire requires more commitment. After the initial burning fire, people often want their partner to do the seducing instead of feeling the awkwardness or vulnerability of stepping up. *They should go first,* we think—and most of us can bet that our partner is thinking the same.

Getting past the nostalgia for and attachment to that initial phase of lightning sexuality creates space for the intense curiosity and commitment required to build a fortified subtle sexual field. Both people need to want their sexual life to mature into multiple dimensions of nuance, allure, and temptation. We have to acknowledge that virility or amorousness need not be measured by how often we have explosive orgasms.

To become lovers for whom sex does not begin and end in the bedroom, we need to have an erotic practice and language that grows more deep and passionate over time. This becomes especially critical when partners go through hormonal changes, illnesses, losses, the demands of children, and all the other seemingly unsexy aspects of life most of us face. Throughout, we safeguard the subtle sexual field to ensure that intimacy is not thwarted by these inevitable challenges.

So next time we watch the hunk throwing a beauty over their shoulder, we can appreciate that Herculean sex move and feel grateful that this image is not the benchmark of a fully expressed sexual life.

ILLUMINATIONS

Here are a few astrology tips to grow your subtle sexual field. These tips apply whether they are your or your partner's Sun signs, Moon signs, or the sign on your eighth-house cusp. You can also look at what sign Mars is in for you or your partner.

Aries: Give and receive head massages while saying sweet romantic appreciations.

Taurus: Bring on the silk and satin in your voice and in your sheet choices.

Gemini: Try a variety of costumes and underwear and entertain each other.

Cancer: Learn the powerful art of holding someone while they share their deepest truths.

Leo: Do new role plays and trade genders if you feel like it.

Virgo: Stroke and caress the arms and legs with ardent admiration.

Libra: Set up a gorgeous scene at home or in nature and make time to hear about your lover's favorite settings for romance.

Scorpio: Make private rendezvous a habit and tell each other your secret desires.

Sagittarius: Go on nature adventures and tell each other what you most appreciate and love about each other's spirits and bodies.

Capricorn: Make a ritual of bathing or showering together with candlelight and scented soaps.

Aquarius: Surprise your partner with hidden love notes and unexpected flowers.

Pisces: Dance slowly and close while listening to a song that turns you both on.

Onward . . .

Sexuality isn't just about sex. If we let it, the energy that under-lies our sexual natures permeates all we are and everything we do. It's the energy of *eros*: life force, development, and growth. When we remain in touch with our erotic selves, everything in our lives becomes more vivid, deep, joyful, and creative.

It can be difficult to bring this powerful energy and vitality into the rest of our lives. We're so *busy*, and so much of life seems so unsexy. It's easy to feel as though this deep and dynamic part of ourselves—the part that is tied in to transformation, death, and rebirth—can't be integrated with other aspects of being alive. We save it for the act itself and partition it off in the rest of our lives.

Changing this habit requires in-tention and practice. It requires a commitment to dipping into the sen-sual and into the subtle sexual field as parts of everyday life. It requires a willingness to risk owning our needs and desires and sharing them with our significant other, and a willing-ness to consider our partner's needs and desires with curiosity and a sense of adventure.

Sensual is everything that refers to the delight of the senses. And that's what artists do, is stimulate the senses in any possible way.

—Shakira (Mars and Mercury in her Capricorn opposed by Moon in Cancer)

CHAPTER NINE

The Ninth Domain: Make-Believe

It is not our differences that divide us. It is our inability to recognize, accept, and celebrate those differences.

—AUDRE LORDE (JUPITER, RULER OF THE NINTH HOUSE, IN LIBRA IN HER FIRST HOUSE)

I recently had an epiphany about the phrase that makes up part of the title of this chapter: "make believe." My associations with that phrase have generally had to do with childhood concerns like fairy tales, Pixar movies, mythological creatures, or the fantasy worlds children concoct when they play. But as I deeply consider what these two words mean when I put them together, I realize that *making believe* is something everyone does, at all ages.

All of our beliefs come down to make-believe—as much as

they may feel like incontrovertible truths to us. They may have been handed down by our families, our ancestors, or our cultures, or they may be direct results of our life experiences; either way, they become so deeply ingrained in us that they feel like facts. We are very good at finding confirmation that our beliefs are true in some absolute sense, and most of us humans find a lot of comfort in having our beliefs confirmed. What I'll maintain in this chapter, however, is that belief is something that's made, not a reality outside of our ability to choose—and that holding this to be true gives us access to vast wisdom, peace, and potential for contribution.

The ninth house focuses on our belief systems and higher learning from life, education, and travel. The sign on the cusp of that house and any planets we have within it reveal how we will approach our beliefs and meaning-making experiences.

Making meaning is unique to the human species. We are perpetual meaning makers. Higher learning and long travel adventures are important spaces for deep inquiry and the creation of meaning maps. In this chapter, we'll focus on how we travel inside and out to make meaning in our lives. We'll also look at the more personal internal ways we make meaning: at the level of our automatic, emotionally driven default belief systems. Our psychological programming around these systems can be upgraded, and we will explore that process, too.

Energy follows thought. What we believe, we perceive. All human beings possess a mental pattern called *confirmation bias*: we look constantly for evidence to reinforce what we already believe. Beyond this distinctly human habit is a truth known through the science of quantum physics—that reality is based on perception. Concrete and absolute objective proof of our beliefs exists only rarely.

To become truly evolved in our meaning making, we can cultivate curiosity about the origins and construction of belief systems other than our own. Where do those beliefs come from? What practices and rituals are involved? What makes them compelling? How are they beautiful and true?

Think for a moment about how differently people could relate and coexist if instead of believing our belief system is superior—which often means fighting for that system and judging or condemning others—we would approach this conversation with the understanding that all belief systems are valid. If we practiced looking for confirmation that all belief systems are ways people manage mystery and the unknown, we could stop arguing over whether one iteration of God is better than another, or whether one philosopher got it right and the others got it dead wrong. Every conversation about belief could become a journey toward greater understanding and connection and a broadening of our own horizons.

It starts with us. Let's explore the ninth domain with this in mind.

Traveling Inside and Out

It's easy to understand how long, adventurous journeys lead to great "aha!" moments and accelerated personal growth. Traveling to foreign lands always involves challenging hours, stressful conditions, and discomfort. Despite all the inconveniences and frequent learning curves, humans have always possessed a desire to go beyond their local realms. There is nothing quite like being out of your cultural comfort zone, propelled into rapturous moments full of new sights, sounds, sensations, aromas, and tastes.

The elements in travel can be exhilarating or daunting, depending on the perceiver and the context. For a friend of mine with three planets in Aries in the ninth house, flying on a massively turbulent flight is fun! For my friend Jaclyn—Taurus Sun and Mars and Venus in Virgo—that same flight means a panic attack.

Not everyone has the opportunity to go on long journeys because of finances or other circumstances. Fortunately, the ninth domain is also related to inner travel. The imagination is a free worldwide pass, and all of us—whether we travel in real life or not—could stand to spend more time engaging in active imagination rather than the passive viewing that has become so commonplace.

Let's turn, first, to journeys through the physical plane, and look at preferences and growth opportunities according to the elements. Considering the ways each sign in the element may flourish on a trip can nudge each of us to try new voyage options.

Assessment: Travel Through the Elements

Look at the travel choices in the following list and underline the ones you have experienced or would most love to experience. Cross out those that seem least desirable. If you are an astrology novice, don't worry about the signs associated with each type of trip—just see what appeals to you most. Your preferences are likely to reflect your Sun sign, your Moon sign, or the sign on the cusp of your ninth house.

 Fire

Badass action and adventure (Aries)

Undertake any type of daredevil activity, like bungee
    jumping or helicopter skiing.

Attend a workshop that includes fire walking.

Play, recreation, games, and childlike wonder (Leo)

Spend time in a magical theme park or on an epic fairy tour.

See the Seven Wonders of the World.

Visit a Ripley's Believe It or Not! museum.

Take a trip designed around musical theater or fabulous
    light shows.

Pilgrimage to a place of deep meaning (Sagittarius)

Visit the Pyramids or Stonehenge, or climb a Tibetan
    mountain.

Undertake any journey that entails connection with
    embodied wisdom. If horses are included, all the better
    (the glyph representing Sagittarius contains the Centaur).

Earth

Sensual luxury and splendor (Taurus)

Stay in a place with five-star, over-the-top luxury and
pampering: only the best and most sensual surroundings.

Surround yourself with splendor, awe-striking views, and
possibilities for picturesque walks.

Acts of service (Virgo)

Build houses for the poor.

Teach English as a second language.

Spend time at a retreat center to work on a project or book.

Go on an ecological mission to save a dying species.

Ambitious goals (Capricorn)

Go on a backpacking expedition.

Take an extreme-weather survival trip.

Take a journey involving certification in some new area of
learning.

Air

Learning and conversation (Gemini)

Attend United Nations convenings.

Go to conventions focused on causes in foreign countries.

Follow big stories or emerging trends on media- or journalism-focused trips.

Take a trip centered on foreign languages, such as a language-school intensive.

Fine art, fashion, design, and style (Libra)

Visit art galleries and museums.

Do anything that has to do with high culture or keeping abreast of modern aesthetics.

Communal activities, community engagement, and rebellious enterprises (Aquarius)

Attend Burning Man or another community-building festival.

Visit the site of an epic world event like the fall of the Berlin Wall.

Take an ayahuasca journey in Peru.

Do anything that has to do with birthing new visions for community, self, and the world.

Water

Great food (Cancer)

Take a cooking course.

Go out for meals with gourmet menus and sommeliers.

Visit cities with a focus on the best spots to eat.

Take a tour with visits to foreign homes that deepen your understanding of food in different environments.

Intense emotional catharsis and profound mysteries (Scorpio)

Visit famous cemeteries or ghost towns.

Visit sites of trauma like the death camps in Germany.

Involve investigations into life's dark side in your travels.

Water (Pisces)

Take riverboat or ocean cruises.

Visit a rainforest.

Bathe in hot springs.

Swim in majestic waters or go waterskiing or surfing.

The Elements in Belief Systems and Inner Exploration

Systems of belief, philosophies, and religions are ways we make sense of our lives. They are based on ideas, which are the province of air. That being said, belief is manifested and expressed across elemental energies. Words and ideas, written or spoken, are air. Rituals, food and drink, and routines or practices are earth. Art, music, and pageantry are fire, and the feeling senses and core emotions brought out by belief systems are water.

People are drawn to religious affiliations and philosophies for different reasons. We might be attracted to one elemental quality of a faith tradition, belief, or philosophy and not to others. Zela says she can't stand some of the old ideas of Catholicism related to divorce or sexuality, yet she is emotionally transported by the singing and rituals of Catholic services. Lauren doesn't enjoy the formality of Jewish High Holiday temple events, but she enjoys special holiday foods and scripture reading at the dinner table. Although Sam calls himself a Buddhist, he cannot bear sitting still in meditation. He does love to listen to Buddhist podcasts, though, and deeply feels the timeless beauty of Buddhist art. Willa is a great student of astrology, yet she has no use for the many online astrology apps that are popular now.

Contemplative practices and inner exploration are important parts of many faith traditions and belief systems. This is where inner journeys join with outer journeys in the ninth domain. Even as we take these kinds of journeys within our current systems of belief, we can use the uniquely human drive toward making meaning to open up our perceptions and discover new ways to see and be in the world. In modern neuroscience, we'd call this *enhancing your neuroplasticity*: challenging your heart, mind, and body in ways that build new connections between neural circuits.

This next assessment will guide you to consider the ways you access meaning through experiences, beliefs, and philosophies, and the inner journeys they have invited you to take.

Assessment: Your Meaning Making

How do you learn? How do you make sense of your life, of your world? As you read these descriptions of meaning making through the astrological signs organized by element, notice which ones resonate with your experience.

Fire

Aries: bodily wisdom

Your most meaningful and revelatory experiences come through movement. These moments may involve victories over your perceived limits of the body: where you ran faster than you thought imaginable; where you pretzeled yourself into a previously impossible yoga posture; or where you had a breathtaking sexual adventure in which your body seemed to transcend all previous limitations.

Leo: the heart

Your most meaningful experiences are those that move your heart to such an earth-shattering degree that you never feel the same again. The birth of a child, the beginning of a romance, the majesty of a sunset, or the exquisite perfection of a work of art make meaning by transporting you to total heart bliss. Cosmic, unconditional love floods your heart chakra. You feel imbued with a sense of divine affection.

Sagittarius: philosophical teachings or spiritual apprenticeship

Perhaps a book has changed your life, giving you a new framework for thought and action. Maybe a teacher who entered your life became a guidepost for your journey, or a sacred learning journey led you to a life path that feels meaningful and right.

Earth

Taurus: sensual enjoyment

Beauty is what propels you forward. Gorgeous art, stunning material or natural compositions, and other aesthetically pleasing experiences—taken in through all the senses—are the rail you use to walk up the stairs of meaning.

Virgo: ritual and routines

You build meaning through activities like prayer, using mala beads, timed meditations, and sacred fasting. Through everyday, essential tasks of worship, you access life's deeper relevance.

Capricorn: exhausting, highly challenging courses that build character

Maybe you put in the grueling work required to complete basic military training; maybe your meaning-making quest is to finish a PhD, or to deeply study a faith tradition or religious text until you achieve the mastery required to teach others about it. The common thread: coming to understand your place in life by submitting to a greater authority with specific, rigorous rules and regulations. This way of making meaning may also involve positions of leadership in the police force, military, or government.

Air

Gemini: ideas and inspirational words

You frame your reality through exploration of the thoughts of the greatest minds in history by way of quotes, books, and speeches. You are lifted up by the eloquence of others, finding your path through profound study of languages, literature, and oratory.

Libra: relationship

You see life's meaning through interrelationship and make more meaning through one-on-one partnerships and couple's work. This is the path of You-and-I as the nexus of awakening.

Aquarius: sudden insights, flashes of intuition, and extraordinary, nonconforming awareness

You see things as whole systems and all the parts as flexible and interrelated. This portal is about accessing "meta" visions of life and seeing things beyond ordinary consciousness. Windows into the future pull this energy forward.

Water

Cancer: compassion, empathy, and emotional release

Through your explorations of caring and sharing, you find that we belong to one another. This is the way of the divine feminine—the great goddess connection where we feel an overarching, tender mother's love for the world.

Scorpio: profound transformation

Experiences like deep losses, illnesses, or betrayals offer you glimpses of your most powerful vulnerability and the eternal nature of human experience. Through surviving unbearable loss, you encounter the permeability of the human spirit. Within that, you rise from the ashes, and you see a deeper meaning at work.

Pisces: channels, mediums, music, and anything arising from the unseen worlds

Through the invisible, you realize we are made of something bigger than ourselves, which is far beyond our reach. As you dissolve into a unitary consciousness for moments in time, you learn about the great and everlasting oneness.

Your Meaning Making: Practice

How do you make meaning in your life? Journal, discuss, or make art around the ways you chose. Include in your reflections the elemental blueprint of your ways of making meaning.

ILLUMINATIONS

The ninth house relates to our belief systems and our quest for meaning in life through travel, education, and embodied wisdom. The planets in your ninth house or the sign on the cusp of that house indicate how you will go about making meaning in your life.

For example, if you have the Moon in the ninth house, your journey in this life will focus on investigating both your thoughts and your feelings. As the Moon represents your relationship to your mother, its placement in the ninth house suggests that your mother was influential in the development of your belief systems. That influence may have been harmonious, where your mother handed down belief systems that feel good and right for you; or it may have been difficult, where your beliefs were formed in opposition to or rejection of those of your mother.

If you have Venus in the ninth house, your belief systems and meaning making are likely to revolve around deeply held values and the pursuit of beauty . . . or, perhaps, your values reflect a preoccupation with shallow concerns that aren't really feeding you or serving those around you, and you could stand to evolve your belief systems and philosophies. If you have Mars in the ninth house, you probably have taken an active and engaged stance—maybe even an unskillfully aggressive one—around beliefs and meaning. Saturn in the ninth house could indicate that you are a builder of systems that provide discipline and structure around the making of meaning . . . or that you are stuck in a belief system that doesn't serve you.

Assessment: Negative Core Beliefs

I have worked with thousands of clients, and every one of them turns out to have basic negative core beliefs that have become ingrained in them as limitations. These beliefs lurk below our conscious awareness, and they dictate our behaviors and perceptions—especially during stressful times. Core negative beliefs correlate strongly with unskillful aspects of each element that were developed through adverse prenatal, birth, or childhood experiences.

Everyone, me included, has these kinds of limiting beliefs about themselves. They usually are founded in the earliest attempts to connect, love, be loved, and freely express ourselves and the almost inevitable rejections and disappointments that are just plain part of being a human being. You can have a basically fabulous life and still lapse occasionally into negative core beliefs. On the other hand, some people find that no matter how much they try, they keep falling into a pit of self-sabotage based on one of these foundational dysfunctional beliefs.

In this next assessment, you'll identify your top three negative internal operatives. This is the first step to recognizing the signs that you are about to fall into negative patterns or expressions based on these beliefs.

Look at the following list of negative beliefs and correctives, which are arranged in element categories. Circle the three negative beliefs you struggle the most with. If you don't immediately know what yours are, consider what element you most identify with and think about how it is most likely to hold your negative core beliefs.

Negative Core Beliefs	Countering Positive Beliefs
FIRE	
I am bad.	I am okay the way I am.
I am selfish.	I can take good care of myself.
I am an asshole.	I can manage my anger.
I am powerless.	I can get help and make changes.
I am a mistake.	I have a purpose here.
EARTH	
I am not enough.	I am good enough.
I am inadequate.	I can learn as I go.
I am damaged.	I am not the mistakes I make.
I am broken.	My past is not my future.
It is my fault.	I can repair mistakes I make.
I am an impostor.	I am capable.
AIR	
I am stupid.	I know a lot and can learn.
I am ugly.	I am divinely made.
I am crazy.	I can trust my perceptions and fact check them, too.
I am an alien.	My uniqueness is part of a divine order.
I can't say my truths.	I can get support to say what I need to.
WATER	
I am unlovable.	There is much to love about me.
I am weak.	I can build my core strengths.
I am not safe.	I can find ways to make sure I am safe.
I don't belong here.	I have every right to be here.
I am helpless.	I can ask for help.

If you are struggling to identify negative beliefs in yourself, try the following process a few times. Set aside a decent chunk of time and ensure that you have emotional support if you need it, as looking at this question clearly can bring an emotional jolt.

1. Bring up an upsetting incident from your life—not something that is too disturbing, but something that was enough to impact you emotionally in a negative way. (An example might be "When one of my adult children said horrible things about me.")

2. Notice what that memory feels like in your body. Notice how intense the charge is. Rate it from 1 to 10, with 1 meaning no charge and 10 meaning absolutely overwhelming.

3. Identify the feelings that go with this memory (sad, mad, hurt, rejected, fearful, frustrated . . .).

4. Write down the negative internal belief about yourself that goes with this incident. Allow it to come not from logical thought but as a primitive response, from the gut. It should emerge in simple, childlike language ("I am bad").

5. To finish, consider this: What would you prefer to believe about yourself? Stay away from the flip side of the coin and look more realistically at an adult correction to that belief: "I am okay the way I am. I am lovable."

Negative Core Beliefs: Practice

Wherever you have circled a negative core belief, look to the corresponding positive belief in the table or develop your own.

Remember not to go to the opposite extreme; choose a realistic adult correction to that belief.

Begin to notice where your negative core beliefs tend to pop up. Counter them with the positives. Say them to yourself; write them; say them out loud; say them to other people. Seek out evidence that the positive is true—in other words, shift your confirmation bias toward positive self-beliefs. Look for the good and you will find it. Notice that the negative beliefs limit your choices; positive beliefs open you up to possibility.

Transforming our belief systems requires practice, just like learning to ride a bike or dance the salsa, or to master a new yoga pose. Negative core beliefs are habitual, and habits take time and intention to break. You are changing deeply ingrained neural patterning. Every time you intervene to soothe yourself with a positive self-belief, you change your brain, and soon that new belief will become your default.

Changing Core Beliefs

Saskia had suffered much abuse in her life. She had developed deep beliefs that she was not safe and that something was wrong with her. Through therapy, supportive groups, and friendship, she came to realize that she could now create living situations and relationships based on emotional safety. Although people had done serious harm to her, that was on them. It did not mean anything was wrong with her. She came to see herself as a survivor rather than a casualty.

Denzel had spent his twenties addicted to drugs, and he had

done horrible things to himself and many others. His negative belief was that he was bad and deserved to die. Through a rigorous self-assessment, a mindfulness practice, and a twelve-step program, he came to understand that he could heal. Through Eye Movement Desensitization Reprocessing trauma therapy, he realized that he had started using drugs because he felt so unloved and worthless in his family. He wanted a way out of his pain. As he uncovered the cause of his early addiction to drugs, he continued to work his twelve steps beautifully. He began to realize that now he was okay the way he was. He could do something positive with his life: he mattered.

Lucia felt ambivalent about her marriage, and this ambivalence plagued her deeply. She recognized that because her mom had cheated on her dad, she saw marriage as a trap that would inevitably lead to painful betrayal. Through reflection, she realized that she had a core negative belief that *she* was not enough and that she would fail. As she began to identify this as a belief rather than a fact about herself, she started to heal and acknowledge that she *was* good enough and could make her marriage a different story. She began to appreciate that she had access to tools and skills for making her partnership work that her mom never had.

Jasmine had a big temper and would explode on the folks she cared about most. For years, she just justified herself, doubling down on her reasons for being mad. Then she looked around and realized she was operating from a core belief: *I'm an asshole, so why not just act like one?* Digging deeper, she found that her anger had been activated early on by a dad who consistently put her down and told her she was selfish when she didn't want to spend time with him. After much therapy and work on her hair-trigger anger, Jasmine was able to extinguish her fuse before she blew. She understood that she was, in fact, someone who deeply cared and wanted to protect those she loved.

Onward . . .

The ninth domain asks us to recognize that beliefs and belief systems are choices we make and not absolute truths. It asks us to be willing to be curious about and deeply consider our beliefs and those of others, and to choose to take advantage of the unique ability of the human brain to remodel and evolve over time. The rewards of doing so are lifelong learning and growth and greater connectedness with the whole human family.

Each element has its own take on how to work the muscle of belief:

> **Fire:** With plenty of stimulating creative outlets and contacts, you'll stay inspired and awakened to your ceaseless potential to expand your beliefs and horizons.
>
> **Earth:** Active resistance is necessary to shift narrow-minded bad habits and behaviors and old traumatic emotional adaptations. It's work to get unstuck from the mud of harmful beliefs, and you are an excellent and hard worker.

Air: Any limited belief can be challenged and upgraded. You have the vision and intelligence to do so at any time.

Water: You need strong experiences of compassion and caring to keep loosening whatever shackles you to outworn ideas or emotional beliefs.

CHAPTER 10

The Tenth Domain:
Legacy and Lasting Impressions

Once you figure out what respect tastes like,

it tastes better than attention. But you have to get there.

—PINK (SHE HAS SUN, SATURN, AND VENUS IN THE EARTH ELEMENT OF VIRGO)

The tenth domain is about character and authority. What is the footprint of our character, and how does it lend us authority? How do we author, originate, influence, and honor the world we live in? What is our impact? How will we bring our unique strengths to bear in making our mark? What legacy might we leave behind?

In astrology, the tenth house is often narrowed down to considerations of career. The truth of this house, and the focus of this exploration of the corresponding domain, is that every one of us has great potential authority. It's about your inner sense of living *your* true purpose, not living the life you think will make others respect you. Authority is possible for everyone, no matter their occupation or social role.

I have a friend named Maggie who has given her life to raising three outstanding children and supporting her husband to rise to the top of his field. Her consistent and focused love as a mom and partner is her authority; her power shows up in creating a real ambience of joy and contribution in her family. I know a table server named Maria who has more honor and impact in her job than most bosses I have worked for. Every time she serves me, I feel as though my presence and enjoyment are singularly important. Her authority is about making others feel special and well cared for.

On the other hand, I've met with many CEOs who are paid extremely well but feel disrespected or even hated. They command others well, but do not inspire them. They lead by fear and intimidation instead of connection. They make big demands without cultivating an atmosphere of purpose, agency, and camaraderie.

As you enter this exploration of the tenth domain, ask yourself at the end of each day: *How would I evaluate the impact I have made on others? How did I—and how did I not—bring out the best in them?*

ILLUMINATIONS

The tenth house in astrology has been largely associated with one's career or reputation. It is the section of the sky that correlates with high noon, and the sign ruler and planets it contains give clues about who we are when we are most prominent and visible to others. Having Aries on the cusp of the tenth house, for example, might mean a forceful, energized, fiery approach to our life work. Scorpio on the tenth-house cusp could indicate that our authority and ultimate legacy will emerge through fierce truth-telling and fearless transformation. Having Venus in the tenth house might reflect that our authority wants to express through the cultivation of beauty and harmony.

Saturn, the archetype of authority and stewardship, rules the tenth house and the sign of Capricorn. If you have planets in the tenth house or in Capricorn elsewhere in your chart, a big part of your life learning curriculum is about the difference between reputation and legacy.

People often come to me for career direction. Any discussion I conduct with a client about career centers on identifying where they feel most useful and most inspired to put concerted effort behind using their gifts and talents.

Here is a sampling of career paths through the elements in the tenth house. Notice what you are drawn to and whether that sense of interest and aliveness translates to the work you are actually doing.

Fire

Aries: firefighter, athlete, professional fighter, activist leader, dancer, attorney, emergency room physician

Leo: creative director, actor, singer, child educator, storyteller

Sagittarius: motivational speaker, travel consultant, spiritual teacher, horse trainer

 Earth

Taurus: jewelry designer, clothing store owner, banker, luxury brand consultant, bodyworker, somatic psychotherapist

Virgo: healer, psychologist, nutritionist, nurse, acupuncturist, chiropractor

Capricorn: political leader, CEO, investment counselor, environmentalist, military leader

 Air

Gemini: journalist, social media consultant, talk show host, writer, communications teacher

Libra: mediator, lawyer, stylist, model, judge, marriage therapist

Aquarius: community organizer, nonprofit executive, documentarian, astrologer, scientist

 Water

Cancer: memoirist, top chef, home designer, childcare provider, food inspector

Scorpio: detective, surgeon, funeral home manager, occultist, transformational leader

Pisces: musician, filmmaker, artist, psychic, magician, hospital administrator

Once we have determined a great career fit for our talents and efforts, what matters most is the way we execute our careers in terms of the use of authority. We can access our inner sense of authority and contribution through the elements.

Part of this process is to look at how we might be taking authority in an unskillful way. Are we acting out behaviors with the goal of impressing others, rather than looking within and expressing what's ours to express? Are we letting societal expectations about wealth or high-powered careers nudge us away from the true legacy we are made to leave behind?

Assessment: Uses of Authority

Review these lists of skillful and unskillful uses of authority. Honestly mark your top three skills with authority; then mark the top three unhelpful ways you tend to access authority.

 **Fire**

Skillful

☐ Protective leadership

☐ Innovative actions

☐ Fearless vulnerability

☐ Responsible risk taking

☐ Open-hearted motivating

☐ Meaningful mentoring

Unskillful

☐ Dominating posturing

☐ Creation of self-serving systems

☐ Reckless management

☐ Egotistical incentives

☐ Exploitive love affairs

☐ Boasting and exaggeration about accomplishments

☐ Use of lying to get ahead

☐ Anger

Earth

Skillful

☐ Solid, reliable decision making

☐ Conserving, caring decision making

☐ Trustworthy, safe mentoring

☐ Long-lasting values

☐ Purveying of beauty

☐ Hard-working egalitarianism

Unskillful

☐ Stubborn, recalcitrant participation

☐ Rigid, righteous lording over

☐ Motivation by greed

☐ Withholding of power

☐ Starvation for recognition

Air

Skillful

- ☐ Setting of vision with a clear directive
- ☐ Inspiring wordsmithing
- ☐ Uplifting positivity
- ☐ Fabulous conversation
- ☐ Witty, humorous repartee
- ☐ Equity-centered leadership
- ☐ Exemplary diplomacy

Unskillful

- ☐ Unreliable truths
- ☐ Scattered and shallow attention
- ☐ Untethered goals
- ☐ Vanity and overconcern with image
- ☐ Eccentricity over substance

 Water

Skillful

- ☐ Kind, compassionate guidance
- ☐ Patient, connected leadership
- ☐ Transparent actions
- ☐ Deep empathy with others
- ☐ Expert question asking
- ☐ Equanimity with feelings
- ☐ Spiritual centeredness and congruence

Unskillful

- ☐ Rule by dramatic feelings
- ☐ Lack of backbone in conflict
- ☐ Escape from reality to cope
- ☐ Underhanded and sneaky actions to get ahead
- ☐ Manipulative requests

Uses of Authority: Practice

This is where we can start to make conscious, concrete changes to how we lead, no matter where we have influence.

Write down your three skillful ways of expressing authority. Consider how you can continue to use them, or do so more fully. Then go back through the lists and write down six skillful assets you did not select but would like to cultivate more. Notice which element categories they come from. Consider concrete ways to bring more of these assets into your daily life. Journal, discuss, or make art around steps you can take to align with your desires to build inner authority.

If you want to take this practice further, try revisiting the assessment lists daily for thirty days. Each time, note assets and unskillful expressions you noticed in yourself that day. Find a creative way to record your answers. At the end of the month, you'll see a reflection over time of how you are occurring in this domain, which will help you know how you want to move forward.

Assessment: Your Legacy

Do you know what you want people to say about you in your obituary or at your funeral? Although this isn't an easy thing to think about, making an honest assessment of how you wish to be remembered can provide a motivating push in the direction of your legacy. Look through these lists of what people might say about someone they care about who has died. Circle or check the statements you would want to be made about you. Resist the temptation to mark them all—who wouldn't want to be all of these wonderful things to the people who remember them?—but select those that feel the most true about you when you are showing up as your best self.

> When people come to the end of their lives and look back, the questions that they most often ask are not usually, "How much is in my bank account?" . . . You find the questions such a person asks are very simple. "Did I love well?" "Did I live fully?" "Did I learn to let go?"
>
> –Jack Kornfield (Sun and Saturn in Cancer)

 Fire

- ☐ I always felt so loved by them.
- ☐ They brought everyone so much joy and appreciation.
- ☐ The best laughs of my life were with them.
- ☐ They lived so fully and inspired me to do the same.
- ☐ I never knew anyone so courageous and fearless.
- ☐ They always had my back.
- ☐ They always did the right thing, even when no one was looking.

☐ They were so spontaneous and creative.

☐ They were so playful and open-hearted, they always made my day.

☐ Their generosity was stupendous.

Earth

☐ They always made me feel calm and peaceful.

☐ They were the most solid, caring person I knew.

☐ I couldn't have lived without their help.

☐ They were always so gentle . . . truly one of the nicest people I've ever known.

☐ They provided so much for so many others, in such a selfless way.

☐ They were the most thoughtful, service-oriented person I knew.

☐ They were competent at everything they did . . . and so humble, too.

☐ They always knew the right thing to say at the right time.

☐ Their presence was so pure and unpretentious.

Air

☐ They always made me feel smart and witty.

☐ They really knew how to connect everyone to each other.

☐ They were the best friend you could ever have.

☐ They inspired a generation with the way they walked their talk.

☐ Their optimism was so supportive to so many.

☐ Their vision of life always left me feeling so much better.

☐ They were absolutely brilliant.

☐ They knew how to make everyone feel like they mattered.

☐ Their uniqueness gave everyone permission to be themselves.

☐ Their beauty was soulful and everlasting.

 Water

☐ They never said a mean word about anyone.

☐ They were the most beautiful soul I knew.

☐ Their kindness was legendary.

☐ I always felt truly cared for by them.

☐ They demonstrated real compassion every day.

☐ They were fearless in facing the hardest things.

☐ They exemplified resilience and hope.

☐ When they walked into the room, you knew things would be okay.

☐ They were the best parent you could have.

What statements did you select? They are your "true north"—the direction of your authentic legacy. Who do you really want to be? How do you want to be remembered? How far are you from full expression of the qualities you want people to remember you for? Take an honest look, because you get to choose whether you double down on the legacy you wish to leave.

Your Legacy: Practice

Create a piece of visual art around the legacy you wish to leave. Imagine it as a memorial art piece for your future departed self. Spend some time journaling or talking with a close loved one about what might need to change in your life to make your aspirational legacy a reality.

It's Never Too Late

It's never too late to commit to the imprint you want to make on people's lives. I have known many people who, later in life, became the person they wanted to be after chasing windmills of money and accolades—and not being happy with themselves—for decades. They slowed down and realized the gold is in the moment of connection, not in the coins . . . or even in the cause.

Jeremy is a billionaire who has been married and divorced twice. He has Moon and Sun in earthy Capricorn in the tenth house of ambition. He has focused for most of his adult life on creating a fortune and treasuring things and ideas, and has not maintained closeness with his children, who are now adults. For much of his life, he lived in his head and not from his heart. After a great deal of deep reflection and inner work, he realized that family trauma he had suffered in his own childhood had made him not want to get too attached to other people. He felt safer and more capable focusing on intellectual and material pursuits. In therapy, he started to melt away the armor that had kept him from deeply connecting with his children. Although he has not changed completely, his goals are now about feeling instead of doing. He is focusing on repairing his relationships with his children, not on creating more wealth.

Gayle is a mother of four and a social service worker, and she lives for her work. She has watery, nurturing mama Cancer on her ascendant and an other-focused Libra Moon. Her Sun in Leo is in the seventh house, which indicates that she finds love and self-expression through the other. She spends each day giving her heart away. Each person who receives her love feels like they've sat under a magical waterfall of compassion. It's a lot for Gayle to give; she is often drained and exhausted and still can't sleep because she is so consumed by concern for the people she serves. Just doing her job and trying to make even a little bit of time for each of her children every day has put her into overdrive. After her mother died, Gayle realized that if she did not step back from her outpouring of giving, she would drown. She decided to take a wellness course and focus on balance and self-care. Now, she leads by example instead of through self-sacrifice.

Leonard is a stay-at-home dad. He is one of the best dads you will ever meet—but he also has deep feelings of inadequacy that he avoids by focusing all his energy on his kids. Lurking underneath his loving exterior are unmet childhood wounds that rise up on occasion as storms of anger, or as pushing people who love him away. As they sense and fear this roiling cauldron of pain beneath his surface, others walk on eggshells around him. Leonard has many planets in Pisces, which gives him unfathomable emotional depth and caring; but where he feels unattended to, those depths become pits of emotional poison. He had a turning point when he faced a crisis he could no longer run from. As he fell to his knees, he finally accepted the help he had needed all along to live out the unexpressed parts of himself. His experience with psychotherapy was so transformative that he eventually returned to school to become a psychotherapist. There, his depth and deep care for others found true expression.

Tania is a motivational coach and physical trainer. She has an athletic Aries Sun in the first house and fiery, meaning-making Moon in Sagittarius. Tania also has Jupiter with Mars in Taurus, which enlarges her appetites for sensuality and physicality. She has spent her adult life in the wellness community, promoting the health of other people. For a long time, she has hidden an addiction beneath a veneer of exemplary self-care practices. The drama of her excess finally collided with her integrity, and she got sober. Her authenticity, humility, and openness about her struggles have allowed her to make an even bigger contribution through her motivational coaching. The thousands who follow her journey know they can just begin where they are, because Tania provides a living example of facing our imperfections with candor and compassion.

Onward . . .

It's common for some part of a person to be so set on *not* realizing their authority that they unconsciously sabotage themselves, holding on to habits or hiding secrets that prevent them from stepping fully into their purpose. It's not that surprising, really, that we would do this, because with authority come risk and responsibility. When we play big, mistakes and missteps are magnified, and we all know that the world we live in is not great about forgiving someone who messes up while stepping into their greatness. Making the choice to live in such a way that we leave the legacy we truly want usually begins with uncomfortable self-realizations, wrestling matches with self-sabotaging habits, or confrontation of secrets we may be keeping even from ourselves; and then, ongoing courage is required to keep choosing that path.

The steps we take toward courageous and illuminating fire, centering and stabilizing earth, brilliant and uplifting air, and kind and calming water will be the contours of the footprints we leave behind.

CHAPTER 11

The Eleventh Domain:
The Sacred Crew

When you fully invest in the four elements in all the previous domains, you begin to fill with a luminous and steady light. The secret to maintaining this warmth and vibrance is your sacred crew—the focus of the eleventh domain.

Your *sacred crew* consists of eight to twelve people who are your go-to allies. They don't have to be super close to one another—they just need to be connected to you. These are people who are aligned with your growth and ultimate fulfillment instead of your old patterns.

You have been on a path of expressing the elements fully in your self-presentation (Chapter 1), your material possessions and resources (Chapter 2), your communications (Chapter 3), your home and emotional intelligence (Chapter 4), your creativity and passion for life (Chapter 5), your self-care habits (Chapter 6), your one-to-one relationships (Chapter 7), your sexuality (Chapter 8), your pursuit of learning, spirituality, and wisdom (Chapter 9), and your legacy and authority (Chapter 10). This eleventh domain brings your evolving mandala of elements expression into a web of community that reflects all the elements, too. As these energies in you merge with those of your carefully chosen sacred crew, the power and joy you hold as a collective grows exponentially.

Yes, eight to twelve sacred crew members is a lot! It's important to have a group this size, because a gathering of eight to twelve is more likely to include folks who land across the elements spectrum. Consider the qualities of people who reflect each of the elements:

Fire **people who . . .**

- have your back
- will speak highly of you when you are not around and speak up for you when others speak poorly of you
- will take a proverbial bullet for you
- believe that "impossible" is code for "I am possible"
- believe that magic is an indispensable part of life

Earth **people who . . .**

- hold you accountable for your word
- do the right nourishing things with you and for you
- can be relied upon and depended on consistently
- are committed to their own health and well-being—and who know that without a healthy body, the spirit cannot fly

Air **people who . . .**

- are willing to host uncomfortable conversations and work through inevitable ruptures
- make you laugh
- inspire you
- hold you and life in a bigger picture of possibilities instead of getting caught up in obstacles or problems

and *Water* **people who . . .**

- are just as available to host your sadness and defeat with compassion as they are jubilant with you when you are succeeding and achieving
- know you are not your past and your old stories
- remind you to be present and that you are a gift
- share their vulnerabilities and authenticity with you and support you to share your truths and buried shame

---

ILLUMINATIONS

Folks who have the Moon or Sun in the eleventh house prioritize friendship as a superpower. Their emotional need for a group of friends is strong, and they identify with their friendship group as an anchor for their sense of belonging. They may be the one to make sure everyone gathers regularly or starts a business together; they're likely to be the one who steps up to plan bridal and baby showers and bachelor and bachelorette parties.

If someone has Saturn in the eleventh house, they may feel real loneliness when it comes to peers. They may have to make an extra effort to maintain close friends. Jupiter in the eleventh house may bring the bizarre predicament of having too many friends and feeling breathless just trying to keep up with all of them.

Many of us have been taught that while group and friend support is a great thing to have, we shouldn't really *need* it. Cultural norms call on us to be strong, self-made people. If we're taking care of business on our end, we might need occasional support—especially if something in our lives goes wrong—but it's on us to right ourselves as quickly as possible so as not to burden anyone. This mythology prevents us from seeking the depth and breadth of group and friend support human beings actually need. We must learn to resist the dominant narrative of the self-made person who relies on no one, and to see building and maintaining a sacred crew as a reflection of relational courage.

Building Your Sacred Crew

In 2019, Evite and OnePoll asked two thousand Americans about their social dynamics. Nearly half said that it was hard for them to make new friends. Although respondents had an average of sixteen friends, they felt only three were lifelong, and had only five with whom they would want to spend time one-on-one. Just under half of the two thousand participants said that shyness or introversion was the thing that most got in their way, and about the same percentage said they wanted to have more friends but weren't sure how to find them. Why and how should we seek out eight to twelve friends? And how do we create the kinds of relationships with those friends that truly match the profile of the sacred crew?

Although amassing this many folks to hold close might feel intimidating, it is essential. This is the size a tribe has to be to ensure that everyone is held up when they need to be, and that no one member is called upon to cheerlead or support others in the group beyond what their endurance or resources allow.

At first, you may identify only two people you can put on your sacred crew list. With determination, you can build the list of your transformative lifeboat partners. There are so many places to find people for your crew: your existing family and friend groups, therapists and healers, book clubs, places you worship, twelve-step groups, creative collaborations, work, classes, singles clubs, Meetup groups, exercise groups. Start to talk to your close people about putting this kind of crew together and what it will mean for all of you to provide this kind of support for each other.

The self-awareness and relational intelligence you've been building as you progress through this book will serve you well as you consider new additions to your "godfamily." Show up vulnerably for these conversations. Tell the truth about what you are seeking and why. Know that you'll probably hear inner voices of self-effacement and shame trying to stop you from making these connections. Fears around rejection, around hurting others and being hurt, are part of this process, and are no reason to avoid the search or to allow yourself to settle for close relationships that aren't really close. Folks who are not interested aren't the right folks. The right people will lean in and be excited to help you invent the exact kind of sacred crew you both need.

Lovingly cultivating a group relationship with conscious allies means saving your own soul while making you indispensable to others—a need every human being has. It is through valuing our profound impact and interconnectedness that we bring true fulfillment to our lives.

Your crew is your lifeboat and your team of survival coaches. When you are doing well, they are thrilled for you, celebrating your every step toward uncovering your true divine nature. When you fail, fall, or get bruised, bumped, or bloodied, they are there to say, "We've got you. We love you. We are here for you."

Celebrating Resiliency with Your Sacred Crew

I first met Miranda about twelve years ago, when she came to me for a reading. At the time, she was in an abusive marriage with a partner who was routinely cruel and mean, and sometimes physically threatening. Her self-esteem was zero. She had some of the elements going: she was an accomplished dancer and performer (fire) and a professional writer (air). Her physical health was not optimal, despite her having some good nutritional and anti-inflammatory practices (earth), but the stress of her marriage, and the loneliness she felt within it, was beginning to make her feel sick. The ongoing trauma she experienced influenced the breakdown of her immune system. She had frequent respiratory and bladder infections and heart palpitations that made her fear she might be dying. What she wasn't allowed in that situation, because she was being dominated, gaslighted, and bullied by her husband, was vulnerability and sensitivity of feeling (water). To remain in this abusive relationship, she had to keep herself numb. She talked about not feeling like she belonged with people who were functional. She was trapped in secrecy and shame with no one to lean on.

Miranda joined a women's group, which provided her access to people who not only prioritized feeling but made socially and emotionally intelligent communication a priority. They made a safe space for her to begin to share what was really going on in her marriage, but didn't let her get trapped in victimhood. As they affirmed her talents, she began to acutely feel the difference between this and her partner's constant erosion of her sense of worth. She kept up the fire and air, dancing, learning, and writing; she kept working on her nutrition. The thing that really shifted was that she became used to a field of compassion, vulnerability, and transparency. She began to reach out to more folks outside of the women's group, calling them to be with her in vulnerable and feeling ways. She divorced the abusive partner and found herself a partner who exemplified vulnerability and sensitivity and who made room for that part of her. In her work life, she chose and committed to a kinship group that fostered her transparency and fallibility every day. They praised and celebrated her creative, emotional, and physical achievements. At last report, through the love and support of this sacred crew, she has stayed committed to self-realization in all four element areas.

Bob's is a more cautionary tale. He made his mark by being one of the top tech guys in the world. Influenced by the logic and visionary air element styles of Joe Dispenza and *The Secret*, Bob was as highly developed as one can be in fire (physical activity) and air (intellectual learning). Although incredibly fit, he would often overdo it with alcohol, which is highly inflammatory and dilutes the good energy of fire and air. Bob also wouldn't allow himself to be vulnerable, needy, or dependent, or to cry. He was underdeveloped in the water capacities of feeling, vulnerability, and tenderness. This became such a pattern that his need to be in control colored his every waking moment. Bob had attained great social recognition and success, but when crisis struck, he became walled off to those closest to him. He had no ability to feel what he felt or to access help from a sacred crew. His highest priority was to remain in power and control, and this meant he was unable to use the crisis as an opportunity for accelerated heart growth and connection. He became so imperious, righteous, and rigid that people didn't want to relate to him at all, which then led him to lean more on alcohol to deal with repressed feelings. This led to the loss of his dearest friends and his professional position.

We all prefer one element over the others, and become masterful in one or two, but if we don't tend to all four, the lopsidedness that results will be problematic . . . and may be our downfall.

Assessment: Groups in Community

Throughout our lives, we have opportunities to make lifelong connections in community or affinity groups, which reflect another relevant facet of the eleventh domain. We usually develop a standard manner of joining and contributing.

Look at the following list. What are your most tried-and-true ways of participating in groups? Circle or check all you recognize in yourself. Notice especially your unskillful expressions.

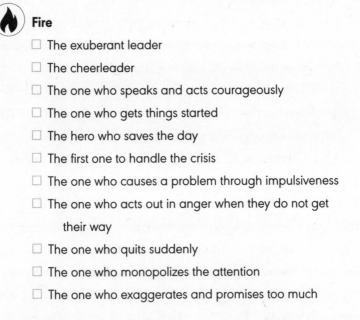 **Fire**

☐ The exuberant leader

☐ The cheerleader

☐ The one who speaks and acts courageously

☐ The one who gets things started

☐ The hero who saves the day

☐ The first one to handle the crisis

☐ The one who causes a problem through impulsiveness

☐ The one who acts out in anger when they do not get their way

☐ The one who quits suddenly

☐ The one who monopolizes the attention

☐ The one who exaggerates and promises too much

Earth

- ☐ The organized leader
- ☐ The detail keeper
- ☐ The accountable one
- ☐ The grounded and sensible one
- ☐ The hard and humble working one
- ☐ The security oriented one
- ☐ The stick-in-the-mud
- ☐ The pessimistic one
- ☐ The forensic, fearful one
- ☐ The one who expects others to do the work
- ☐ The one is who is caught in nostalgia

 Air

- ☐ The inspiration of the group
- ☐ The visionary
- ☐ The wordsmith and articulator
- ☐ The provider of witty intermissions
- ☐ The one with a positive mindset
- ☐ The one with a balanced perspective
- ☐ The one who asks great questions about relevant topics
- ☐ The distracting one
- ☐ The dilettante
- ☐ The unreliable airhead
- ☐ The untruthful one
- ☐ The one who flees when the work is too hard

💧 Water

- ☐ The heart of the group
- ☐ The compassionate leader
- ☐ The one who notices the feelings
- ☐ The one who tends to morale
- ☐ The one who helps others feel safe
- ☐ The quiet, kind presence
- ☐ The one who is needy for nurturing
- ☐ The one who is constantly seeking acknowledgment
- ☐ The one who plays victim
- ☐ The one who sucks the life out of the room with moodiness

Groups in Community: Practice

Consider the expressions you circled, and where on the elements list you found the most that are true for you. Spend time journaling about or discussing expressions you could enhance or hone that are outside your predominant element.

Onward . . .

Group life is fundamental to our existence. For a group or community to function at an optimal vibration, we need participants who elevate all four elements. Without bold leadership, a strong foundation, breadth and inspiration, and a field of empathy and caring, groups inevitably fail or cause damage.

Now that you've recognized how you show up most of the time in your groups and identified ways you might become a more effective contributor, seek to encourage others. Notice their elemental makeup in the ways they tend to show up skillfully or unskillfully in groups. See where they shine and reflect what you see back to them. With your sacred crew, discuss how each of you can polish your group participation and become more conscious in your roles in uplifting and enhancing group life.

CHAPTER 12

The Twelfth Domain:
Spirits and Temptations

The twelfth house in astrology is known as a *bucket house*. It addresses many issues related to the unseen worlds and how they affect us, and is the last house before the beginning of the zodiac. This sector reflects issues of high sensitivity: mental illness, medical institutions, addictions, psychic abilities, musical and artistic talents, spirituality, and service. It also reflects guardian angel energy and the fortune that comes from devotion to spirit. In this chapter on the twelfth domain, we will focus on ways to increase your sensitivity and spiritual fortune.

ILLUMINATIONS

People who have more than two planets in the twelfth house are called to give themselves to humanity in a profound artistic or spiritual way. If these energies are not utilized productively, they can become overwhelming and disturbing.

Many clients of mine who have struggled with addiction have planets in the twelfth house. This suggests that they could not handle their extreme sensitivities early on and found relief in forms of escape. Leaders in the recovery movement have learned how to manage these sensitivities on behalf of the collective. They also find that through service to the idea of oneness, they become more healed in the process.

Kevin, a young man I know, is a good example of this. He began an intense struggle with addiction while still in his early teens. He has the Moon in Aries in the twelfth house, and his loving mother struggled with mental illness (the Moon in the natal chart represents relationship with one's mother). With a great deal of support and guidance through high-quality rehabilitation programs, as well as strong willpower and drive thanks to his twelfth-house Aries Moon and Aries rising, not only is he healed (at this writing, he is almost six years sober) but he has dedicated himself to working with, supporting, and inspiring others in recovery.

In this chapter, we'll look first at how you connect to the divine of your knowing. How do you stay deeply connected to spirit, in a space where you breathe in rhythm with the universe? Then we'll consider how you develop and recognize your psychic abilities, and explore how these abilities matter in the quest to live a fully expressed and aligned life.

This first assessment targets ways we can access the divine of our knowing and the ways we cut ourselves off from it. Today, all of us live with more anxiety and depression than ever before. The constant noise and distraction of our digitized lives short-circuits the antennae we need to divinely connect and receive. Start by identifying five key new ways you can tune into the divine. As you mark this list of ways you connect to and disconnect from the divine of your knowing, you may notice a new invitation to bolster the power of these spiritual antennae. I find that the more elements I apply to my cosmic relatedness, the more gently and steadily my life goes. Now it's your turn!

Assessment: Access Points

Circle or check all the activities you like to use to help you access your divine nature:

Fire

- ☐ Singing
- ☐ Dancing
- ☐ Sex
- ☐ Creativity
- ☐ Intense physical exertion
- ☐ Spontaneous games and play
- ☐ Hysterical laughter

Earth

- ☐ Yoga and sacred herbs
- ☐ Nature
- ☐ Animals
- ☐ Eating
- ☐ Touch
- ☐ Silence

Air

- ☐ Meditating
- ☐ Breathwork
- ☐ Mind-expanding medicines
- ☐ Reading
- ☐ Writing
- ☐ Conversation
- ☐ Prayer

Water

- ☐ Bathing
- ☐ Heart opening assisted therapies
- ☐ Swimming
- ☐ Ocean
- ☐ Catharsis
- ☐ Flow
- ☐ Empathy
- ☐ Compassion

Access Points: Practice

Discuss your favored ways to feel divine connection with a trusted member of your sacred crew, or journal or make art about it. Set a timer for twenty to thirty minutes before you begin and surrender fully to the memory of that connection, allowing your expression to flow from that place. Include lots of juicy details about what you do and how it feels in those moments. If you make an art piece, hang it up in a place where you'll see it often, to remind you of that connection.

Assessment: Vices

Our chosen strategies for checking out and escaping tell us a lot about where our elements are out of balance. Vices are an important part of being human, and are as natural as breathing; we can each feel whether our vices are serving as harmless, temporary pleasures or sacraments or shackles that restrict our connectedness to the divine.

Circle or check all the vices you turn to when you feel disconnected from spirit:

Fire

☐ Temper tantrums

☐ Alcohol

☐ Driving fast

☐ Daredevil feats

☐ Hooking up

☐ Selfies

☐ Affairs

☐ Constant travel

☐ Theft

Earth

☐ Weed

☐ Food

☐ Oversleeping

☐ Couch potato behavior

☐ Consuming

☐ Cleaning to excess

☐ Hoarding

☐ Embezzlement

Air

- ☐ Social media addiction
- ☐ TV bingeing
- ☐ Talk radio or podcast obsession
- ☐ Amphetamines
- ☐ Porn

- ☐ Image obsession
- ☐ News addiction
- ☐ Mushrooms
- ☐ LSD
- ☐ Scamming

Water

- ☐ MDMA
- ☐ Romance addiction
- ☐ Codependency
- ☐ Self-harm

- ☐ Drowning in feelings
- ☐ Manipulating
- ☐ Playing the victim

Vices: Practice

Discuss the vices you circled or checked with a trusted member of your sacred crew, or journal or make art about them. Which of them do you dip into occasionally, without any sense of being overtaken? Which can become damaging obsessions that separate you from your higher self?

If any of your vices are addictive or harmful, it is essential that you seek professional help. When I was in my early twenties, I was depressed, had an eating disorder, and contemplated self-harm. When I reached out to get help, I found that anything can be worked through with enough support and expert care. Having a vice that won't let you go and that interrupts the health and joy of your life is not okay. I have seen hundreds of clients turn their lives around once they realized there was no shame in admitting they were in trouble and needed help.

On the other hand, we all have vices that niggle us. They are mere annoying reminders that we are imperfect works in progress. Beginning to see how vices are substitutes for full-body happiness and health, we can take them on a bit at a time and find new ways of addressing the unmet psychological and emotional needs underneath them.

Fostering Your Psychic Abilities

Many people ask me to help them recognize or develop their psychic aptitudes. It makes sense that they would entrust me with this desire, as I believe—based on experience—that everyone is psychic to a degree, and that they can work on their innate precognitive abilities to enhance and utilize those psychic abilities more fully.

There's a lot of skepticism about psychics, and I will say, it's entirely true that some psychics are frauds. It's also true that many people misuse their abilities to tap into parallel worlds. My desire here is not to support or promote these kinds of bad actors; it is to support *you* in plugging into collective consciousness. I'll trust you to use your newly found gifts for good and not illicit gain.

Why should we seek to become more presentient—to see, feel, hear, or know things before they happen? Exercising this ability helps us to ride the cosmic tide of life with a stronger paddle. It harmonizes us with the rhythms of the universe. Tapping into our psychic strengths is a practice of divine alignment. For example, Fatima tells me that she always knows when her sister is about to call, because she gets a certain tingle in her left ear. Journey shares that before any big rainstorm, he sees a raven in his dreams, flying through a rainbow. Elaine gets the feeling of a punch in her gut before someone she loves is about to get sick. Robbie will hear a particular song play in the car just before some lucky thing is about to happen.

> If it's the Psychic Network, why do they need a phone number?
>
> —*Robin Williams (he had Sun, Moon, and Mars in the psychic water signs)*

This kind of presentience is within every person's reach. Tapping into it is a comforting reminder that we are part of something that transcends the known.

ILLUMINATIONS

The signs and planets you have in your twelfth house will give you a clue as to how to increase your psychic powers. For example: Suzu has Saturn in Scorpio in her twelfth house, and she has found incredible psychic openness through rigorous study of ancient and mysterious enlightenment texts.

Lala has the Moon in Gemini in the twelfth house, and spends a great deal of time imagining talking with trees and fairies. She comes away from these imagined conversations with profound psychic wisdom. Tasha, who has Venus in Taurus in the twelfth house, works with sacred incense and gorgeous aura sprays to expand her psychic channel.

✦

Assessment: Psychic Abilities

Here are a few element-specific ways to tap into your inner psychic hotline. As you read through the list, circle those you already experience. Underline those you wish you *could* experience but haven't yet.

 Fire

A song speaks to you in such a visceral way that the lyrics seem to be sending you a message.

You feel a powerful burning or tingling that seems to command you to slow down and ask what's going on.

You keep breaking things, or things break around you—signaling that it's time to stop and ask yourself, *What I am not paying attention to?*

You keep bumping into the same person for no particular reason and you start to wonder: *What message do we need to give each other?*

You feel a sudden calling to go somewhere and do something for someone. You check it out and realize that the person you are called to is in need of your help or your love.

Earth

You get a solid feeling in the pit of your stomach that you
  need to be more aware of your environment and become
  more self-protective.

You are drawn to a specific place in nature that is like a
  healing touchstone. Your body and soul immediately
  relax and renew while you are there.

Just before you take a bite of food, you get that the food is
  not right for you at the moment—and so you refrain.

When you hug someone, you pick up lots of sensory
  vibrations that inform you about what is going on with
  them.

You have an uncanny relationship to animals; they seem to
  anticipate your every move and serve you in specific and
  telepathic ways.

 Air

When you sit down to write, the words fly through you onto
  the page.

Soon after you hear certain expressions in your mind,
  someone else says the exact words you were thinking.

You somehow know that something great (that you didn't
  order) will come by mail . . . and it shows up.

Certain words leap from the page to tell you about
  something that is about to happen.

You often find that at a certain time of day, you and a loved
  one were having the same thought about each other.

You know weather patterns are approaching before they are announced.

 Water

You suddenly have feelings in your body that are not your own, and realize you are picking up on someone else's emotional state.

You have dreams about things that happen the very next day.

You keep remembering someone from the past . . . and then they show up.

When you sing or dance with someone, you can somehow feel exactly how they feel, what they care about most, and how they will move next.

When you are with someone, you can feel their malady or illness in your body as if it were your own, and this may help you to support them in finding the modalities for healing.

Psychic Abilities: Practice

Now that you've made note of psychic abilities you already have and those you wish to cultivate, bring curiosity, mindful attention, and reverence to your day-to-day life, opening yourself up to more resonance with unseen energies. Share about psychic synchronicities you experience with members of your sacred crew. Notice yourself learning to recognize the difference between a true psychic hit and the fantasies and mental stories we can concoct out of anxiety, paranoia, or a delusional wish phenomenon.

Building Your Psychic Abilities

There are many joyful ways to increase your psychic "muscle." I like to guess at playing cards with friends or guess which card will show up next at the top of the tarot deck. Sometimes, when I am driving and listening to a certain radio station, I'll see if I can guess the next musical artist they'll play. A group of friends and I like to join together to make wishes and keep track of what comes true. Keeping your psychic hotline open for business is best accomplished by (a) knowing you have this capacity and (b) playfully leaning into its energy and letting it carry you. The more you practice this skill, the more proficient you will be.

Here are some tips to cultivate your psychic abilities through the elements:

 Fire

When you are facing a dilemma and don't yet have an answer, take a brisk walk or run (without any distractions piped through earbuds . . . leave the headphones at home). Ask your divine nature to provide you an instant hit of knowing by the time you finish exerting yourself.

When you feel stuck and want to access your intuition, try vigorously shaking your body—in a safe and contained way—until you move the energy into a new vibration.

Sit by a fireplace or firepit and stare into the flames. After a
bit of time, once you have lost yourself in the flames, ask
that they reveal to you a deeper knowing. It will come.

Light a candle as you seek a particular answer to a question.
Let it burn safely overnight. When the candle has burned
all the way down, feel in your gut what the answer is.

 Earth

Sit quietly under a tree. Focus intently on drawing grounded
knowledge from the earth.

Ask an earnest question from your divine intuition. Wait and
listen for a gentle confirmation.

Create an altar for your ancestors. Add whatever feels right
as an offering: flowers, stones, sticks, other precious
objects. Write a note thanking them for positive foresight
and guidance. Once the altar is complete, ask these
ancestors a question and trust that answers will come.

Plant something in your garden, or somewhere in your
neighborhood: a tree or any other plant. Invest in this
seed as a seed of your growing psychic abilities. Visit this
plant consistently; care for it as it grows. It will become a
touchstone for your own growing intuition.

Prepare a special food especially for your psychic guides.
Make this food with extra love and attention. Make every
nuance of preparation a ritual of reverence for your
growing clairvoyance. As you consume this sacred feast,
feel it as a sacrament to your intuition. Repeat this as

often as necessary to become more confident in your gut's true knowing.

 Air

Every morning write a letter to your divine guides, specifically thanking them for their assistance. This activity alone has vastly increased my psychic skills. It must be done daily to be effective.

Get a deck of tarot cards. I like the mythic tarot deck, but any will do. Every day, pick a card about your current state of being. Then ask what will improve that state and pick another card. The mere act of learning the cards and asking for mystical direction will increase your psychic sensibilities.

Keep a couple of books about developing your intuition on your nightstand. Every night before you go to bed, read a chapter. The habit of thinking about psychic or intuitive abilities will prime your capacity.

Looking for signs in nature is a great way to enhance your psychic skills. Hold a question lightly in your heart as you take a quiet walk in a wild natural place. Ask to be shown a sign that will help you answer that question. Keep your eyes peeled for a visual sign; listen acutely for an aural sign. You will be amazed at how nature will reveal insight.

Water

Take a shower or a bath and hold a question in your heart. Imagine the water as a fountain or lake of divine wisdom. Let the water dissolve your mind into a warm feeling in your body. Allow the felt sense of this merging to provide you clarity. Be receptive; over time, water will guide you to soft and true answers.

Crying is one of the best methods to clear the way for intuition. If you become expert at crying, you can tap into vast psychic knowledge. It helps to cry with a loving witness present. Many people shy away from tears because they anticipate never being able to stop or complete the intense grief they sense within themselves. Let me reassure you that if you learn to completely let go and sob till you are through, you can clear tremendous blockages to your divine intuition. Ask a question before you begin your crying catharsis; once you have fully released the emotion, ask the question again. You will have a new view.

Pick a glass to be your sacred portal glass. Thoughtfully, slowly, drink pure, clear water from it at a certain time each day. As you sip, imagine that each drop enhances your emotional clarity. Ask a question before each glass. Over time, your feeling sense of things will grow and deepen.

Use an aura spray or essential oil to open up your third eye chakra center. When you bring concentrated, relaxed attention to that central point between your eyes and above the bridge of your nose, you accentuate your psychic antennae. The ritual of bringing soul-opening scents to this sensitive doorway to perception heightens your innate ability to see things clearly. If you do this consistently and with patient faith, your inner vision will expand.

Onward . . .

How do you get locked away from connection with the divine? You can recognize disconnection by the empty feeling it brings—where you find yourself starving for substances or objects to fill your well. To nourish your twelfth domain, keep noticing where you are checked out or wanting to check out. Keep exploring what works for you to plug back into endless divine sources.

All access points to psychic knowing can fortify our faith, our clarity of action, and our expression. All of these ways of knowing are available to you, regardless of your elemental makeup. To the degree you practice each of them, your alignment will grow stronger and more resilient. Regardless of how you work at this psychic channel, the more energy you focus there, the more and more you will feel tapped into the magical rhythms and continuum of life.

Magic, after all, is really just the gorgeous recognition of the extraordinary in the everyday. It is living in a mindset of miracles, and that life is happening not to us, but for us.

FULLY SELF-EXPRESSED:

FINAL THOUGHTS

This book is an exploration of the elements through twelve different domains of experience.

If you have worked each chapter faithfully, you will have done a deep dive into incorporating fire, earth, air, and water elements into

> Your self-presentation
>
> Your core values and self-worth
>
> Your communications
>
> Your home and personal environment
>
> Your love life and your creative expression
>
> Your health and daily habits
>
> Your partnerships and support language
>
> Your sex life

Your inner and outer travel and meaning making in life

Your legacy making

Your affinity or friendship circles

Your spiritual access and temptations, and psychic abilities

Bringing all the strengths of each element into these domains provides constant jolts of positive energy and vitality and offers you the opportunity to live a fully expressed life.

Life is never static or predictable. Daily practice is required to stay engaged in a whole and robust expression of ourselves in changing contexts. When your battery is low in any one area, you can use this book to remind yourself of your optimal choices and possibilities. Ideally, you will engage your friends and loved ones in this book's discovery process so that you have a common language and road map to support each other's blossoming and sustained learning.

Socrates famously said that the unexamined life is not worth living. Said this way, his statement represents only the perspective of the mind or the air element. I would humbly propose an edit that incorporates all four elements: that the fully expressed life is worth every effort and stumble.

We are here for but a brief flicker in time. Why leave anything on the table?

APPENDIX 1

Understanding Your Natal Chart

A natal chart is an abstracted "snapshot" of the solar system, viewed from the perspective of your birthplace at the specific moment of your birth. It shows the placements of significant astral bodies within the signs of the zodiac, mapped across the sky. At first glance, a chart's symbols and geometry might appear like a cryptic puzzle, but once you understand the meanings of the glyphs and the ways they're positioned in the structure, you can interpret a chart as a cosmic script for your unique personality and life path. Your natal chart holds a tremendous amount of information about traits that remain relatively constant throughout your life. An astrologer reading your chart will not only talk with you about those traits, but also glean intel about you *in the current moment* by looking at the ongoing movement of the planets in relation to the still points in your birth chart.

To understand how a natal chart works, we will use heroic Rosa Parks as an example. The reason I picked Rosa Parks is that her courage had a profound impact on my young life in terms of influencing my education as a young activist for civil rights. Rosa Parks showed me that one person who is willing to stand out can make a difference. Her dignity, her poise, and her devotion to equity have inspired and guided me.

Though charts can be created using a variety of styles and systems, every chart is shaped like a wheel and divided into twelve sections. These sections are called *houses*. The first house begins where you would find the "west" arrow on a compass, where "1" is marked on Rosa's chart. From there, the houses continue sequentially in a counterclockwise direction, with the twelfth house ending where the first house begins. The lines drawn between houses, like spokes of the wheel, are called *cusps*, clearly delineating where one house ends and another begins.

Each house encapsulates a particular realm of life experience. The seventh house, for example, is the space of partnership, while the fourth house is the zone of home and family. Together, the houses are the settings and stages across which the chart's story transpires.

Within the houses, you'll notice a scattering of symbols. Every symbol represents a planet. You can think of planets as the characters in the play, each one embodying its own motivations and goals. In some charts, the planets may be widely dispersed, while in others—like Rosa's—they might be congregated mostly in a certain house or two. Don't worry if some of your houses are

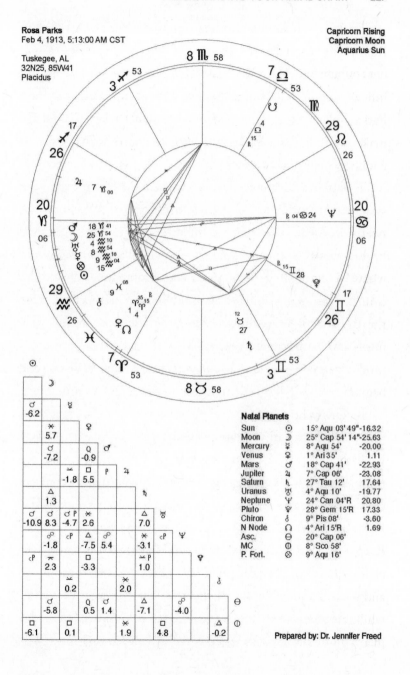

Rosa Parks
Feb 4, 1913, 5:13:00 AM CST

Tuskegee, AL
32N25, 85W41
Placidus

Capricorn Rising
Capricorn Moon
Aquarius Sun

Natal Planets

Sun	☉	15° Aqu 03' 49"	-16.32
Moon	☽	25° Cap 54' 14"	-25.63
Mercury	☿	8° Aqu 54'	-20.00
Venus	♀	1° Ari 35'	1.11
Mars	♂	18° Cap 41'	-22.93
Jupiter	♃	7° Cap 06'	-23.08
Saturn	♄	27° Tau 12'	17.64
Uranus	♅	4° Aqu 10'	-19.77
Neptune	♆	24° Can 04'R	20.80
Pluto	♇	28° Gem 15'R	17.33
Chiron	⚷	9° Pis 08'	-3.60
N Node	☊	4° Ari 15'R	1.69
Asc.	⊙	20° Cap 06'	
MC	Ⓜ	8° Sco 58'	
P. Fort.	⊗	9° Aqu 16'	

Prepared by: Dr. Jennifer Freed

"empty." The crowded houses are simply the ones where a lot of your life's action takes place!

The Sun and Moon are considered two of the key astrological "planets," sometimes called the *luminaries*. Compared to the rest of the solar system, the luminaries progress relatively quickly from one zodiac sign (and house of your chart) to the next. The Moon changes signs every 2.5 days! So, the Moon and Sun placements are fairly specific to a particular birth chart, laying an important foundation for the rest of the story. (Of course, it's Earth that orbits the Sun, not the other way around. Any time we talk about astrological planets "moving" between signs and houses, we're really talking about the *appearance* of movement from our grounded vantage point.) The Sun represents your core identity and vitality, while the Moon represents your emotional needs and distinct feeling nature.

Next to consider are the *inner planets*: Mercury, Venus, and Mars. Mercury helps explain how you think and communicate, while Venus shows how you connect and relate. Mars embodies the specific flavor of your assertive drive.

Jupiter, Saturn, Uranus, Neptune, and Pluto are considered the *outer planets*, switching signs slowly enough that their placements influence generations rather than individuals alone. Jupiter is about luck, abundance, and growth; Saturn is about restriction and hard-won wisdom; Uranus is about rabble-rousing rebellion; Neptune is about spirituality and dreams; and Pluto is about death and rebirth.

Some planets can also be qualified as *benefics* or *malefics*. Jupiter and Venus are considered benefics, bringing positive, pleasurable energy, while Saturn and Mars, the malefics, are seen as more disruptive and exacting. But of course, no planet is simply good or bad—all planetary energies must be used wisely.

In the key provided at the bottom right of Rosa's chart, you'll see a list of the planets with their symbols. This chart and key also include the Mean Node (or North Node), an important point in the Moon's orbit that relates to purpose and destiny, plus Chiron and Lilith, two asteroids that might be taken into consideration as representations of an inherited wound and the shadow side of personality, respectively. Looking at the key, can you find each of the planets in Rosa's chart and see which houses they're in? How many planets are in the first house? How many of these are inner planets, and how many are outer planets?

You'll also notice that there are lines drawn across the chart with symbols on them, from one planet to another. For example, there's a line between Rosa's natal Moon (in the first house) and her natal Neptune (in the seventh house). These lines are used to demonstrate *aspects*: specific angles between the planets that might instigate friction or cooperation between their energies. A *supportive aspect,* in which planets tend to work peacefully together, might be a *conjunction,* when two planets sit at the same degree in the same sign; a *sextile,* when two planets sit 60 degrees apart; or a *trine,* when two planets sit 120 degrees apart. A *challenging aspect,* in which planets tend to confront each other with their conflicting aims, might be an *opposition,* when two planets sit 180 degrees apart; or a *square,* when two planets sit 90 degrees apart. With any of these aspects, you can give or take 2 or 3 degrees, but the closer the planets are to these precise angles, the more potent the effect of the aspect. The line between Rosa's Moon and Neptune shows the opposition between these planets, placed directly across from each other in the wheel of the chart. The line between her Moon and Saturn shows a 120-degree trine.

To truly comprehend a chart, we have to look not just at planets and houses, but at signs. While planets are celestial bodies, *signs* are whole swaths of the sky in which the planets are placed, perpetually progressing forward (and backward, during retrogrades) at their own particular speeds. By seeing the house that a planet is in, we can understand the context or area of life the person will be dealing with that planetary influence, but we need to know the planet's sign to see how it will express itself there. Signs are like the planets' costumes and plotlines.

To see the zodiac signs in Rosa's chart, look around the outside of the wheel. Each one of the large symbols is a sign. As you know from having read this book, each astrological sign is characterized by one of the elements. Aries, Leo, and Sagittarius are feisty, active fire signs. Taurus, Virgo, and Capricorn are grounded, pragmatic earth signs. Gemini, Libra, and Aquarius are intellectual, cerebral air signs, and Cancer, Scorpio, and Pisces are emotional, intuitive water signs.

The signs can also be categorized by mode. The cardinal signs come at the start of a season: Aries for spring, Cancer for summer, Libra for fall, and Capricorn for winter. The fixed signs occupy the middle of a season: Taurus for spring, Leo for summer, Scorpio for fall, and Aquarius for winter. Finally, the mutable signs come at the end of a season: Gemini for spring, Virgo for summer, Sagittarius for fall, and Pisces for winter. You can guess their symbolism accordingly: cardinal signs are focused on the energy of starting, while fixed signs carry the stubbornness and stability to see things through, and mutable signs are skilled at adaptability and change.

How do you know which sign rules each house? Let's use the fourth house in Rosa's chart as an example. The cusp of the fourth house—that line just before the number 4—intersects with the section of the outer wheel that's marked with the glyph for Taurus. The end of the fourth house intersects with the segment of the outer circle that's labeled Gemini. Even though her fourth house ends in Gemini, it's considered "ruled" by Taurus, since Taurus is on the cusp. This house is thus ruled by the Taurean earth element.

Do you see the symbol for the planet Saturn in Rosa's chart? Find the tiny line that marks its precise degree in the circle, showing that it is placed within the fourth house and also within the zone of Taurus. Rosa's natal Saturn is in Taurus in the fourth house, ruled by the earth element. All of this information—house, sign, and element, as well as the mode—helps us understand how her Saturn shows up.

Anyone born on your birth date and year will have most, if not all, of their planets in the same signs (and thus elements and modes) as you. For example, everyone born on February 4, 1913, like Rosa, had their Sun in Aquarius. But anyone born a few hours after Rosa might have had their Aquarius in the twelfth house instead of the first. Someone born around noon would have had their Aquarius Sun way back in the tenth house! This is because of another crucial part of the birth chart: the ascendant.

The signs are always organized in the same order, moving counterclockwise around a chart as the houses do, but to know which comes first in your chart, you must know your birth time, which reveals the zodiacal region that was ascending in the sky as you emerged on Earth. For this reason, the sign that aligns with the first house of the chart is called the *rising sign* or the *ascendant*. Born at 5:12 A.M. on the fourth of February, Rosa had Capricorn rising. (Do you see where the cusp of the first house intersects with the section of the outer wheel that's labeled with the glyph for Capricorn?) Her Capricorn Moon falls within the first house, as does her Aquarius Sun, since most of the sign of Aquarius is in her first house as well. But someone born at 8:00 A.M. would have been a Pisces rising, with their Capricorn Moon in the eleventh house and their Aquarius Sun in the twelfth house. These planetary placements provide for some substantially different interpretations. If you go to a free chart creator on a site like astro.com and plug in Rosa's birth date and location but experiment with different birth times, you'll see all the different ways that the houses of her chart could have turned out, even with her planets in the same signs.

Now we will look at Mila Kunis's birth chart. I chose Mila because I know her and she is a shining example of a chart fully expressed and a great story about post-traumatic growth and the

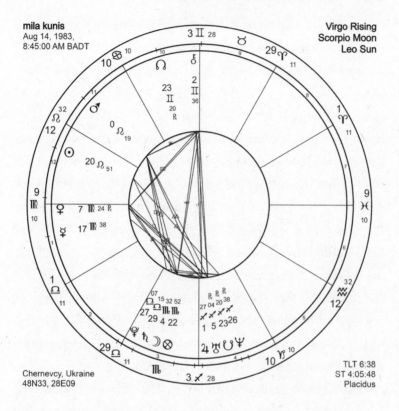

mila kunis
Aug 14, 1983,
8:45:00 AM BADT

Virgo Rising
Scorpio Moon
Leo Sun

Chernevcy, Ukraine
48N33, 28E09

TLT 6:38
ST 4:05:48
Placibus

possibilities of living a heart-centered and wildly adventurous life.

As we examine each of the houses, signs, and planets, and the ways they aspect one another, we can begin to see how the chart provides a map for the beloved star's specific personality and path.

Take a moment to orient yourself to Mila's chart. Remember, you can start at the spot where a compass would point west to find the cusp of the first house, otherwise known as the ascendant or the rising sign. You'll notice that Mila's ascendant is the sign of Virgo, marked by the 9 at the left center line of the chart that sits on the outside ring.

Virgo is a mutable earth sign, oriented to service, precision, and practical smarts. As a Virgo rising, Mila comes off as both clever and humble with a sharp sense of reason. To know more about the "mask" she wears in her first impressions, however, we have to consider the important astrological aspect happening right at her ascendant. The benefic inner planet Venus is positioned at 7 degrees in Virgo, the same degree of the same sign as the cusp of the first house. Venus brings beauty and relational skills right to the surface of Mila's demeanor, embodied through the exquisite discernment and meticulous perfection of Virgo.

There's another important planet in Virgo and in the first house, too: Mercury, about 10 degrees past Venus. This is the planet of communication, so it imbues Mila with a propensity for intelligent articulation in her day-to-day life.

Look closely, and you can see that the cusp of the second house hits just slightly before the final degrees of Virgo. So, Mila's second house is technically ruled by Virgo, too, though it is mostly occupied by the cardinal air sign of Libra, the next sign of the zodiac. In Libra and right toward the end of the second house, we find Pluto. Since Pluto is one of the outer planets, its zodiac placement isn't hyperspecific to Mila but instead marks her generation—all people born between 1972 and 1984—with the power and responsibility to transmute "me" to "we." With Pluto in the second house, we might expect Mila's most potent metamorphoses to be tied to her physical possessions, values, and resources, which are second-house themes.

Moving on to the third house, of communication, we find two more important planets: Saturn in Libra and the Moon in Scorpio. Saturn is all about responsibility and restriction as the building blocks for maturity, so wherever we find it in the chart, we see a special capacity for mastery if proper grunt work is done. With Saturn in Libra in the third house, Mila is called to develop hard-won expertise in beautiful, harmony-promoting storytelling.

With the Moon in the third house, Mila's emotional well-being is anchored in the transmission of ideas and narratives, too, but we must also consider its placement in fixed and watery Scorpio, known for its deep wells of emotion and its magnetic prowess. Aren't Mila's acting accolades making more and more sense?

The fourth house, ruled by mutable, fiery Sagittarius, is the most crowded one of Mila's chart. Here we find three of the outer planets and discover some insights that align with her ancestral history and upbringing. Mila was born in Ukraine to a pair of Holocaust survivors, and when she was seven years old, her family moved to the United States to pursue more promising job opportunities and to escape the anti-Semitism in their small Ukrainian hometown. With Jupiter, Uranus, and Neptune all in the worldly and adventurous sign of Sagittarius and in the fourth house of family and home, we might expect to find themes of both volatility (Uranus) and expansive possibility (Jupiter and Neptune) in Mila's roots.

In the next five houses of the chart—the fifth, sixth, seventh, eighth, and ninth, as we keep making our way around the wheel in a counterclockwise direction—we don't see any planets. This just means that these zones of life are perhaps less energized than the others, but we still have to look at the signs ruling each house to understand the qualities that occupy them.

Mila's fifth house is ruled by the cardinal earth sign of Capricorn, which infuses her creative projects and modes of self-expression with industrious ambition. (It makes sense that she's a leading actress, not a sidekick!)

Her sixth house is ruled by the fixed air sign of Aquarius. This imparts her acts of service and daily work with quirky humanitarian values.

Her seventh house, of partnership, is ruled by the mutable water sign of Pisces. With its sensitive and dreamy tendencies, Pisces makes Mila's relationships feel transcendental. Her eighth house, of intimacy, is just barely ruled by Pisces, too, instilling that same sort of imaginative permeability in all the ways she exchanges energy with others.

Her ninth house has cardinal, fiery Aries as its ruler. In all travel, learning, and boundary-breaking exploration, Mila possesses the assertive confidence of the sign of the ram.

By the tenth house, we find Chiron and the North Node, both in the mutable air sign of Gemini, which also rules this house. Here, again, we see the importance of communication in Mila's chart, this time through the chatty, curious sign of Gemini in the zone of the chart that relates to career and public callings. With the twins as its symbol, Gemini has a natural gift for wily duality, and the North Node points to destiny, while Chiron points to healing abilities through this acting-appropriate talent.

The eleventh house is ruled by the compassionate and caring cardinal water sign of Cancer, but as it transitions into fixed, fiery Leo, we find Mars, instilling an assertive drive (that's Mars) to perform (that's Leo) and a passionate sense of personality. The eleventh house is the chart's most social zone, so this placement might explain why you can often find Mila gracing red carpets and special events.

Finally, we arrive at the twelfth and last house to find Mila's Sun, which is located at 20 degrees in Leo (the house's ruler). The twelfth house is associated with the deep corners of the mind and the unconscious. Perhaps it's no wonder that Mila excels as an actress, since she can access her brightest sense of self within the psyche, allowing her to capture the nuances in identity through her professional roles.

For a full understanding of the complexities in Mila's chart, we must also look at the aspects, the meaningful angles of the planets in relationship to one another. You'll notice a number of lines drawn between the different planets, but let's home in on one of the strongest—meaning that the degrees of the aspect are especially precise—and most significant. Find Mila's Moon at 4 degrees in Scorpio in the third house, and then follow the line to Venus at 7 degrees in Virgo. These two planets are approximately 60 degrees apart, so they are sextile. This is a supportive aspect that allows the astral bodies to collaborate with one another, and since Venus is a benefic, this is an especially positive omen, providing Mila with a particular charm and gentle sensitivity.

Then, find Mila's Sun at 20 degrees in Leo and follow the line to Neptune at 26 degrees in Sagittarius. These planets are about 120 degrees away, which makes the aspect a trine. When Neptune, the planet of dreamy inspiration, trines the Sun, we can expect great creative and artistic inspiration, channeled intuitively.

Each and every one of these components of her birth chart helps to paint the full picture of Mila's individuality. The more planets, signs, aspects, and houses you consider, the more information you get. But when in doubt, scale it all back to just the Sun, Moon, and rising sign, and you can see how Mila channels the passionate heart of her Leo Sun through her Virgo rising to serve collective good, all rooted in the emotional depth and transformational ability at the core of her being, thanks to her Scorpio Moon.

Your Chart

Now, when you are looking at your chart, the rising sign is also worth considering on its own. If the Sun reveals an individual's conscious personality and the Moon conveys a quieter internal identity, the rising sign demonstrates an outward embodiment of these energies. It is sometimes described as the "mask" or the house of first impressions, because it's an important clue to how we are seen by those around us in our day-to-day lives. Someone with a bold and ambitious fire-sign Sun might appear more grounded and humble by way of an earth sign on the ascendant. A cool, calm, and collected rising sign in the air element might belie a more sensitive water-sign Moon.

Over the course of your lifetime, you might find that your relationship with your rising sign changes. As you learn to own your Sun and Moon more visibly, the guise of the ascendant begins to fall away, revealing your true needs and desires in public. Or you might discover a multitude of ways that you embody the rising sign's qualities through a wide range of experiences and roles you play. All of the placements in your chart, in fact, might seem to take new shape as you evolve, learning to grow into the wisest, most evolved versions of the opportunities that your chart's general script presents.

On the next page, find a worksheet you can use to begin exploring your own chart, which you can download for free at astro.com. First, you'll take note of which house is ruled by which sign and which element, with particular attention to the first house (the ascendant). Then, you'll find all of your planets and record which houses, signs, and elements they're in, starting with the essentials: the Sun and Moon. If you don't know your birth time, you can just enter "unknown" or 12:00, though this won't reveal your rising sign or the accurate placements of planets in the houses, you'll still be able to see the sign that each planet is in and thus the element that rules it.

Worksheet

My **rising sign** (on the cusp of the first house) is _____, ruled by the element _____. Here are the ruling signs and elements for all of my other houses . . .

HOUSE	RULING SIGN	RULING ELEMENT
2		
3		
4		
5		
6		
7		
8		
9		
10		
11		
12		

My **Sun** is in the sign of _____, ruled by the element _____.

My **Moon** is in the sign of _____, ruled by the element _____.

Here are the houses, signs, and elements for all of the other planets in my chart . . .

PLANET	HOUSE	RULING SIGN	RULING ELEMENT
Mercury			
Venus			
Mars			
Jupiter			
Saturn			
Uranus			
Neptune			
Pluto			

The Houses: Key Words and Phrases

The astrological houses represent twelve departments of life or fields of experience. In the birth chart, they tell us where the planetary action is taking place.

First House

Ruled by cardinal fire Mars

How you project yourself in the world and how the world perceives you

Second House

Ruled by fixed earth Venus

What you value and what you think you have

Third House

Ruled by mutable air Mercury

How you communicate and what is said; siblings, short trips, mental habits, neighbors, writing

Fourth House

Ruled by cardinal water Moon

Your roots, origins, home and family; also the ending of your life

Fifth House

Ruled by fixed fire Sun

Self-expression, how loved you feel, romantic love, children, love affairs

Sixth House

Ruled by mutable earth Mercury

Mind, body, spirit, reevaluation of your internal world, daily routine, apprenticeships, service

Seventh House

Ruled by cardinal air Venus

Relationships with others, one-to-one partnerships, the other, your perfect other. The sign on the seventh house is what you need to complete yourself.

Eighth House

Ruled by fixed water Mars

Sexuality, death, and taxes; mysteries, what is dark and hidden; how you experience death

Ninth House

Ruled by mutable fire Jupiter

Quests, finding meaning through journeys, higher education, long trips, trips to find the soul

Tenth House

Ruled by cardinal earth Saturn

Striving in the public domain, public accomplishment, what you achieve, and how you are viewed in your public arena

Eleventh House

Ruled by fixed air Uranus

Experience of friends, being part of groups, communal energy, the importance of friendships and your community, humanitarian causes

Twelfth House

Ruled by mutable water Neptune

Institutions, escapes, spiritual influences, muses, addictions, psychic abilities

House Systems in Astrology:
Placidus versus Whole Sign

A common question from inquisitive astrology beginners is *Which house system should I use, Placidus or Whole Sign?* Many astrologers have taken a strong stance in favor of the Whole Sign house system, believing that it is a powerful tool that carries more historical merit. But plenty of astrologers state their preference for the Placidus system because of their familiarity and comfort with it. My approach uses the Placidus system, but the Whole Sign system has gained enough popularity that I wanted to address them both here. Both systems have strengths and weaknesses for astrological interpretation.

Placidus

Because of its interpretational nuances, I find the Placidus system to be more supportive of psychological astrology—where the focus is on reading the chart as a map of individual development and actualization.

The Placidus house system, like the Whole Sign system, divides the birth chart into twelve houses, and they are not all the same size; they can range between 25 and 45 degrees. In all birth charts using the Placidus system of house division, the first house will start where the ascendant (the Sun's horizon line) begins. This can mean that more than one astrological sign falls within a house: for example, the fourth and fifth houses might both fall within the zodiac sign Sagittarius, and the sign Capricorn may be intercepted within the fifth house; or the tenth and eleventh houses might fall within the sign Gemini, and the sign Cancer may be intercepted within the eleventh house. Some of the astrological signs might not rule a house on their own—a feature that provides more subtle distinction to a birth chart.

Zodiac sign interceptions can reflect psychological energies that need to be worked with and brought out, and this is why the Placidus system is a better fit for individual astrological readings. Astrologers who work with sign interceptions find that they can signify how a zodiac energy may express itself in unawakened or indirect ways and can help their clients learn to strengthen them.

For example: in a birth chart where the first house starts at 29 degrees Pisces and the second house begins at Taurus at 3 degrees, Aries will be intercepted and sandwiched between the

Pisces and Taurus. Because no astrological house cusp falls in the sign Aries, an individual with an intercepted Aries in their birth chart will have a harder time recognizing and utilizing Aries energy. This piece of interpretation is lost in the Whole Sign system.

The chart's ascendant is where the first house begins. Aside from the *ascendant*, there are three angles found within the birth chart: the *descendent*, *imum coeli*, and *midheaven*. In Placidus system, the fourth house of home, family, and heritage begins at the imum coeli's starting degree; the seventh house of close relationship begins at the descendent's starting degree; and the tenth house of legacy and reputation begins at the midheaven's degree.

Whole Sign

The Whole Sign system is the older and better known. Much information about the Whole Sign system was lost since its adoption by Western astrologers during the Middle Ages (between the fifth and late fifteenth centuries), although most of this information was restored during the 1980s and 1990s, and the system gained popularity during the first two decades of the twenty-first century. The Whole Sign system can be easier to use once an astrologer has located the ascendant, and astrologers using it can avoid the complexities involved with interpreting intercepted signs.

Where the Whole Sign system is applied, the twelve houses are divided evenly among the zodiac signs. Each astrological house will fall entirely into one of the twelve zodiac signs, so that every sign rules one of the houses. In the Whole Sign system, each house will start at 0 degrees and end at 29 degrees, which often results in the chart's ascendant falling either on or ahead of the first house (between 1 and 29 degrees). Astrological angles (ascendant, descendent, imum coeli, and midheaven) are floating points within the astrological houses rather than fixed on the cusps of the first, fourth, seventh, and tenth houses.

For astrologers who write horoscopes, the Whole Sign system proves more convenient; houses equal in degrees make general astrological forecasting easier. When an astrologer is interpreting for an individual as opposed to creating generalized horoscopes for each zodiac sign, the Placidus house system may be preferable, because the first house of self begins at the ascendant's degree and makes possible much more specificity and detail.

Onward . . .

One of the distinct differences between these two house systems is that Whole Sign is preferred in Eastern (Indian) society, while Placidus is preferred in Western (North American and English) society. Differences between these cultures—that of the individualistic, self-focused West and the more collectivist East—can impact the ways astrological charts are interpreted in these parts of the world. I like to say that whenever an astrologer gives a reading or creates a horoscope, it is *a chart reading a chart*: the biases of the astrologer always impact the way charts are read. In addition, every individual's identity exists within a larger cultural context, and that context impacts the way charts and horoscopes are interpreted and used by those receiving readings. The choice between the Whole Sign and Placidus house systems is affected by all of these factors.

Wisdom can be gained through both the Placidus and the Whole Sign house systems. These systems function best when utilized intentionally, meaning when the astrologers take into consideration what type of information they are trying to derive from a birth chart. The Whole Sign system may be best when working to attain an external perspective of the birth chart and for predictive astrology. The Placidus house reading can be most helpful if the astrologers wants to be more precise and look more deeply into the psychological nuances of the client.

References

Hand, Robert. *Whole Sign Houses, the Oldest House System: An Ancient Method in Modern Application.* ARHAT Publications, 2000.

Kahn, Nina. *Astrology for Life: The Ultimate Guide to Finding Wisdom in the Stars.* New York: St. Martin's Press, 2020.

APPENDIX 4

Precession of the Equinoxes

Why People Say Astrology Is Not Valid Anymore . . . and Why They Are Wrong

The argument of the Precession of the Equinoxes is frequently made by those opposed to astrology, who claim that it "disproves" astrology. Because of the Precession of the Equinoxes, the zodiac signs do not now correspond with the constellations that share their names.

The point referred to by astronomers as the "vernal equinox," and by astrologers as "0 degrees Aries," is in fact seen each year from the Earth as slightly before its previous year's position against the background of the constellations. This is because of a wobble in the Earth's axis, caused by unequal gravitational pulls of the Sun and the Moon on Earth's surface. The point referred to as "0 degrees Aries" is now actually seen from Earth in the constellation Pisces.

"Aha!" the skeptics say. "That proves astrology is nonsense. You can't say that someone's sun is in Aries when that point in space is now in Pisces, right?"

Wrong.

Much confusion arises for the layperson because the constellations have the same names as the signs of the zodiac, but they are not the same. The groups of stars marked on charts as constellations are not actually groups at all. What we see from Earth is the pattern of several sources of light, some from millions of light-years away, and others from much farther than that. These "groups" have no definite boundary lines, but are classified by humankind into constellations.

At the time these constellations were being named and their names becoming known, the 30 degrees of ecliptic starting from the vernal equinox was called Aries, and the constellation that appeared as its background was therefore also called Aries. No precise date can be given for this naming, but the Precession of the Equinoxes was not discovered until 134 B.C. by Hipparchus.

It is the vernal equinox point (0 degrees Aries) that appears from Earth to move farther back each year. The constellations remain in the same positions. However, the signs of the zodiac are and always have been counted in 30-degree segments from the vernal equinox point. Aries will always be the first 30 degrees of the ecliptic (with the other signs following on) and therefore will, each year, appear slightly farther back against the background of the constellations.

So the fact that the point we call 0 degrees Aries is now seen from Earth as being against the background of the constellation of Pisces has nothing whatsoever to do with astrology. It neither proves nor disproves anything. When people assume that it somehow "disproves" astrology, they have not understood the difference between the astronomical constellations and the astrological zodiac.

It might help you to think of the signs of the zodiac as a kind of shorthand to describe the various degrees of the ecliptic (remember, this always begins at the vernal equinox, and its starting point does not change). Each 30-degree segment of the ecliptic has certain astrological significance, but we don't actually need to call them Aries, Taurus, and so on. It is just easier to say (for instance) that in a particular chart Mars is at 3 degrees Cancer rather than have to say it is at 93 degrees of the ecliptic.

More Astrological Exercises by Sign

Although these exercises are organized by zodiac sign, take up any that speak to you. Remember that every one of these signs is part of your natal chart. These exercises are meant to increase areas and elements you are already strong in and to address elements and areas you need to bolster. Perhaps you are working to balance a natal chart that has a lot of a particular element; you could feel drawn to the exercises for that element, and could use them to hone or amplify its positive expression. Or you could gravitate toward balancing exercises characterized by other elements.

Aries (fire)

Deep inside, each of us has a fearless warrior for love to be remembered and cherished. At this book's writing, the Aries ram in us is asked to push through our indifference and excuses to stand up for those who have been marginalized or oppressed.

We are only as great as our weakest parts. It is the fuel and fire of brave Aries that can motivate us to move beyond inconvenience and self-interest to call forth the best of our human natures. The new heroes are moved to act in a web of interrelatedness and bravely lead by acknowledging others' strengths and contributions.

One person can and will be the tipping point; it might as well be YOU.

Pick one cause that you are going to relentlessly work for. How will you speak about it, act on its behalf, and put your money where your mouth is? Pick only one, so your incredible personal influence and agency can make a lasting impact.

Taurus (Earth)

When we see "things" as temporary pleasures instead of being proof of our measure, we naturally choose to be generous and gracious in sharing what we can. For the best qualities of Taurus to come out, we need to focus on cherishing the Earth more than shiny objects, and treasuring our true and loyal friends more than seeking other better offers.

Take stock: What is ENOUGH? What is excess? What will it take to clean up this planetary mess?

Contentment is holding true to long-term values and emotional and material sustainability. Each of us has a part that wants more and more time, money, and relationships, and forgets that having is not the same as appreciating. Whatever we have at this moment is ours to take care of and be grateful for.

So today, give something away. It could be a phone call. It could be a big check. It could simply be sharing a meal.

Whenever we give to others who have less love, time, money, or access, we take a step in the right direction.

Gemini (air)

Many of us under the spell of Gemini tend to overcommit, overspeak, and overindulge in rapid digital responses. In order to bring sanity to our brains and bodies, we all need to remove chatter from the menu. When we adjust our expectations to reality, without losing steam for a bigger dream, we come into mature alignment with what is and the potential of what will be.

Spend more effort on reflecting, reconsidering, and finding quiet in nature. To calm our nervous systems and keep important promises, we need to find the stillness that is here, waiting to be heard.

Adopt speaking prudently and walking the integrity track of thoughtful communication as a daily practice. Emphasize reasonable speech and reflective digital behavior. Take five

minutes to do nothing but look at nature and ask this question: What do you most want to say to me?

Cancer (water)

In Cancer, opportunities for vulnerable and powerful communication expand, and you can become even more radiant in your quest for authenticity.

This is a time to ask for your needs to be seen and understood, and it's all about revealing what is underneath that protective shell of yours in a kind and authoritative way.

Nurturing transforms to be about structuring and maintaining clear boundaries, instead of capitulating to manipulative emotional demands or ploys. Remember, loving someone does not mean sparing them any hurts necessary for their personal growth.

These are gold rush days if the gold you are seeking is your soul. It's time to ask for what you want and need!

Today, practice by telling at least two people something you would like them to do for YOU. Keep it simple and doable. Let them know what it will mean to you that they attend to you in this way.

Notice: How does it feel to speak up for your needs?

Leo (fire)

Leo invites personal expression in relation to others' contexts. Creativity and affection will be modified in each situation through the realities and terms of others in the field. The humility required is to be clear on the greater love vision and to keep chopping wood and carrying water, no matter what detours come your way.

We can learn a lot by not getting attached to any one moment being the prophet of the next. Choose to be true-hearted, even as you navigate bends and twists in the road. The heart will always refine according to what it finds.

What is something you want or wanted, but haven't received exactly when you wanted it? This may have been frustrating, but now's the time to see it from a new angle.

Write to a friend today and tell them how your character has been made stronger by things that haven't gone precisely the way you wanted.

Do you see the strength you've cultivated when you've had to let life unfold in its own way? Remember that the path is unfolding perfectly and imperfectly at all times.

Virgo (Earth)

Virgo energy is about drilling down to the essences in a field of expansive acceptance. It's about

> staring at ants building their hills while feeling the light
> > breeze in your hair
> playing with grains of sand and listening to the lapping
> > waves

holding the gaze of a beloved with rapt attention and
touching their hair with tenderness

Use the analytics of Virgo to become more fascinated with all the ways in which details are gateways to timeless and formless dimensions of love. Through precise awareness and openness, we encounter the infinite.

Choose a particular living detail to focus on. Truly behold it with utter devotion. At the same time, allow the energy around your body to expand into the greater divine. Notice the depth and breadth of the beauty of this moment.

Libra (air)

As we slip and slide from the intensity and demands of our lives and of the world, Libra asks us to constantly breathe and consider: "What is my center point now?"

The scales are always tipping in favor of rebalancing. If you involuntarily go down a rabbit hole of extremes, see how gently and quickly you can right yourself. Leave no room for self-judgment.

Practice by walking on a ledge, edge, or line that is very safe. Keep noticing what it takes to walk clearly and purposefully. Take time to enjoy the feeling of rebalancing.

Are you able to catch your balance? How does it feel?

Scorpio (water)

Have you ever noticed that it is in the darkest solitary moments of night that we encounter the rejected, denied, or silenced parts of ourselves?

We are all called to look at the censored shadows in ourselves and others. Scorpio challenges each of us to befriend and tend our deepest concerns and self-loathing into buried diamonds wanting to see the light. In the still of a dark moon, we learn what we have silenced within ourselves.

The soul knows no division between dark and light, and it is our sacred task to embrace ourselves and attend to the most un-loved parts with more fervent compassion and diligence.

Take some of your nighttime scenarios, thoughts, or feelings and write about them as though they're the most important stories to tell.

How do they call to your heart to be healed, forgiven, or acknowledged? What can you learn from listening to your shadow?

Sagittarius (fire)

Whether you are in love or pursuing your career dreams or wishes for the world, holding tight to a future outcome robs you of the pleasure and presence of the process.

When we are hunting and pursuing a goal with a black-and-white lens, we become more focused and rigid. Sagittarius helps us see that it is better to imagine an ideal experience of love or peace you would like to have, and then to release it to the divine of your own knowing.

Freedom is found through letting go of outcomes.

Write down three aspirations on a piece of paper. Burn the paper while saying: "I release all dreams to the divine of my own knowing, and I become a joyful, disciplined player in the unfolding of life."

Do everything with joyous determination to elevate love and creative expression in your work, personal life, and in the world; at the same time, treasure every curve in the road.

How does it feel to let go of outcomes and enjoy the adventure of now?

Capricorn (Earth)

Change the guard from one of domination, competition, comparing, and blaming to one of protecting, nurturing, stewarding, and being accountable.

This is the year to stop bullying and start bolstering. Instead of "blowing it up," "killing it," or "nailing it," lean into befriending, tending, and accepting it.

Find a place in your life where you have been incessantly driven by feelings of inadequacy. Sit down with a friend and ask them to simply listen to you speak about where your mind is unkind to you. Resist any urges to turn to fixes; instead, let someone hear and hold the distress of the comparing mind. Soften around the comparison virus. Just feel the connection between you and your friend.

See how much better it feels to connect than to compare?

Aquarius (air)

The sign of Aquarius represents the beloved weirdos of the world. We all need to embrace our outrageous quirks more than ever.

As the old ways fight to resist inclusion, diversity, and direct paths of knowing, it will be imperative for all closeted healers and seers to come out of the closet. It is time for the freaks, geeks, soothsayers, oracles, and magicians to become more visible. The future is not what we have known. It is what is at hand, and it is how we show up with an all-embracing plan.

Do something outrageously affectionate or kind for someone who would least suspect it.

The more we can demonstrate outrageous connection and creative manifestations, the less lonely the planet will be, and the more folks will realize we do not live in a dead universe. The world is begging for your magic and acts of unreasonable generosity and love.

Pisces (water)

We are all flawed. We are all broken somehow and somewhere. We all have been hurt and we have all hurt others. Pisces reminds us that there is no superhuman you or me. The grandiose, inflated urge to be beyond others is simply sad and misguided.

The most impressive people I know admit their flaws consistently and celebrate others constantly. When we realize that we are truly not below or above anyone, we release all pressure to be a way that we are not.

With openness and tenderness, find the parts of you that have been held hostage to the "up/down" narrative and greet them with a warm embrace.

There is no remote place inside ourselves to which compassion cannot speak.

Write to someone you trust about the two flaws you have been ashamed of and the two attitudes of being better than others you would like to let go of.

Let's get back to this motto: "Everyone do what you can, when you can, to leave this world better than you found it."

More Astrological Exercises by Planet

Reality and imagination are not opponents. Science and faith are actually two sides of the same coin; both are fervent inquiries to discover meaning. During this continuing time of unprecedented adversity, we all need to find strength and resilience beyond what we had imagined. This is what defines character and history. We can learn from each planetary archetype how to evolve our divine possibilities and move into a positive and realistic mindset.

Sun

The Sun represents our true source of light, the battery of our soul. When our Sun is fully expressed, we are a beacon to others. It is identity merged with authentic essence. It represents an urgent invitation to become a better version of ourselves.

Saying "thank you" to everything and everyone who supports your life is a powerful way to fortify your essence. Every day, I write a note to thank the divine of my knowing and to request guidance. Write your own words of gratitude for whatever has been given to you, and ask to be shown the way through this day with peace and gratitude. Here's a recent note I wrote to the divine:

> *Oh Divine, thank you for my health and well-being*
> *Thank you for the shelter and the clear seeing*
> *Thank you for the bursting beauty of nature*
> *and teaching me to be emotionally mature*
> *Show me how to receive and nourish my soul*
> *Show me how to be noble and whole*
> *Show me how to believe and perceive the beauty and the time-*
> *   less*
> *And be loved in my completeness*

Write a thank-you to the divine each day. Notice how much light enters your body.

Moon

The Moon represents our innermost needs and our divine plan for nurturing ourselves and others. It is a true and unblemished guidance system that resides within us.

On the outside, we wear clothes and social masks; on the inside, we host innumerable, ever-changing needs and feelings. Often, our exterior presentation fails to reflect the exquisite complexity of the dark and light commingling inside us.

Today, notice how aligned your presentation of Self is with your inner knowing and needs. Write three statements about what you truly need today. For example: *I need time for myself. I need time outside in nature. I need to remember to breathe deeply when I get scared.*

Notice that these statements are not about what I need from others. Those needs are secondary to the needs I can attend to for myself. Becoming master nurturers to ourselves is the first step toward emotional fulfillment.

Mercury

Mercury represents how we think and communicate. What we say to ourselves and in the world has profound effects on the energetic field. Notice how angry and hateful words hurt the body. Notice how fearful words create anxiety. Notice how loving words light up the body, mind, heart, and soul.

What is the energy your words put into the world? We all need to vent sometimes, but many of us are unconscious about the amount of toxic communication we dump on ourselves and others.

Today, make a point to breathe before you speak, and to breathe before you berate yourself. Reset after the breath and ask yourself, *How would I like to be remembered?*

Often our impulsive speech is not that skillful. Take time today to speak words that inspire and uplift. Also take note of any pearls of inspiration you spoke aloud today.

Venus

Through the archetype of Venus, we learn about our values and the style in which we prefer to relate.

How often do we align our relationship choices with our core values? If transparency is your core value, do you lead with that, or do you wait for others to share first? If kindness is a priority, do you maintain that even when aggravated on a marketing call?

To begin to consciously choose to align your values with your actions—to be the one to *lead with the love you want to exist in the world—write down your five core relationship values. Do you most value humor? Respect? Affection? What values are most important to you in your intimate bonds?* Keep these values present in your body today. Consider them your to-dos. In every text, Zoom call, or chore, notice what happens when you prioritize these five values as the precedent for your behaviors and words.

Mars

Mars relates to our capacity for action, assertion, and aggression. It is about right action: doing what is best, no matter who would ever know, approve, or disapprove. Some of us have hotter tempers than others. Some of us quash our temper and get paralyzed with depression. Some of us excel at asserting our needs and wants. Do you know where you stand, in terms of how you access your active energy? Let's evaluate.

Rate yourself from 1 to 10 today in terms of using your energy skillfully. 10: You are physically fit and emotionally assertive. You are an engine of effectiveness and clear action. 5: You are off and on again with physical activity. You build up resentments because you only assert yourself when you have had it. 1: You are physically inert and emotionally wimpy. You let others boss you around and you collapse when you set goals for yourself.

No matter where you place yourself on the Mars scale, improve your Mars energy by doing something great for your body, even if just walking around the block a few times. Also, make one clean, assertive statement about what you need. Make sure everything is stated in neutral terms without blame.

Jupiter

With Jupiter, we learn the right use of abundance, and we tackle the search for meaning. When we expand our worldview and apply belief systems that elevate ourselves and others, we feel more emotionally full. Jupiter magnifies whatever we use our energy for, and enlarges the subjects we think about. It reminds us that love is always the high road.

Today, imagine a world in which you are free from doubt and act upon your highest principles. Think of one situation or relationship in which you have played small because you have limiting beliefs. Just for today, do something in that situation that shows you believe in yourself and that love is a bigger power than fear.

Saturn

Saturn is our yoke to this world. It reminds us that we came to this life to do something important. With Saturn, size does not matter—but intention does. Discipline on behalf of altruistic inspiration is true manifestation.

When we do not do our part in developing our talents and possible contributions to this world, we feel like crap. Saturn rules depression; when we resist our callings out of laziness, self-worth issues, or avoidance, we become depressed. So, today, be honest about one small thing you can do to raise your energy level toward health and well-being.

What is your one small thing? Do this thing every day this week and tell one trusted other about what difference it makes.

Chiron

Chiron teaches us that all of us have ineffable wounds that will never heal, but that will instruct us if we allow them to. The message of Chiron is to tend our wounds so we don't inflict them on others, and to perhaps teach others what we have learned in our own healing. When we realize that we are never above or beyond anyone else in terms of needing to learn lessons, we can eagerly reach out to others to help us mend our ways and feelings.

Today, your assignment is to take one of your greatest wounds and rename it as your gift. For example, one of my greatest wounds is not feeling emotionally understood by my parents. This became my quest and my life work: at the root of psychology and psychological astrology is the understanding of others and myself.

Take one of your painful truths and see it as a portal to your gift. Anything hurt and wounded in ourselves becomes a gift of healing light when treated with constant and true love.

Uranus

With Uranus, we learn what it means to be disrupted from our torpor and awakened from our unconsciousness. Sometimes with Uranus energy we feel like we have been struck by a thousand volts of electricity; and other times, it can be like seeing a sunrise for the very first time.

Assume that most of the time, we are somewhat checked

out—on automatic. Enter Uranus, which governs our original spark of creativity, originality, and shocking revelation.

Today, set a timer to go off every hour and use it to call you to attention. Keep brief notes about what you wake up to. *What do you think? How do you feel? What is it like to take a moment with yourself to be fully alert and alive?* Uranus's influence can resemble suddenly falling in love or being slapped rudely across the face and told to WAKE UP. Choose today to fall in love with the wake-up bell.

Neptune

Neptune reminds us that we are all fundamentally particles and waves, and not one of us escapes the ultimate unifier: death. The illusion of our separateness also creates a false sense of hierarchy and protection. As we all know, a pandemic can kill anyone. A bad night's sleep is indiscriminate. Anyone can be deceived. Anyone can experience bliss.

Neptune teaches us that all of humanity is bound by our common experiences of laughter, tears, love, and suffering. The trick is to dissolve into this boundless knowing as often as possible to recognize how precious are our brief, flickering lives.

Poetry, music, and the arts are all under the spell of Neptune; they help us enter into states of formlessness and timelessness. So today, pick one of your gateways to the timeless. Choose a transporting form of expression and purposely honor the unknowable magic of what lies beyond human realms.

What did you learn by leaving time behind and fully entering the now? What if you were dialed in to that frequency more often?

Pluto

Pluto reminds us that we are here to be reborn over and over again and to let the shells, defenses, and false beliefs go. It tells us: Let your false self die a thousand times if it means just one true glimpse of who you really are.

Deconstruction is never pleasant, but sometimes the rot just has to be thrown out. The important thing is how we rise from the ashes of our past with resolved emotional courage and authenticity. I like to make the suffering count. Why bother going through emotional crucifixions if there are no learnings to pass on?

Review the times in your life that somehow you have experienced an ego death—for example, I might include when I did not get chosen for the PhD program I first applied to in my twenties. List two of yours here. Then consider: *What did those ego deaths and real-life disappointments teach you? What part of you died in those situations? What part of you was born out of that loss?*

I realized that the program that had rejected me was too conservative for the path I was on. I had to start over and eventually found my way to a PhD program that furthered my true self.

RECOMMENDED ASTROLOGY
BOOKS AND WEBSITES

Use Your Planets Wisely by Jennifer Freed

Astrology for Yourself: A Workbook Approach to Learning the Basics by Douglas Block and Demetra George

Chart Interpretation Handbook: Guidelines for Understanding the Essentials of the Birth Chart by Stephen Arroyo

Key Words for Astrology by Hajo Banzhaf and Anna Haebler

Llewellen's Daily Planetary Guide by Paula Belluomini and Michelle Perrin

The Twelve Houses: Exploring the Houses of the Horoscope by Howard Sasportas

World Ephemeris: 20th & 21st Centuries by Robert Hand or at www.astro.com

Psychological Astrology

The Astrological Neptune and the Quest for Redemption by Liz Greene

Astrology, Psychology and the 4 Elements: An Energy Approach to Astrology and Its Use in the Counseling Arts by Stephen Arroyo

Astro-Psychology: Astrological Symbolism and the Human Psyche: The Traditional Wisdom of Astrology Examined in the Light of Jungian Psychology by Karen Hamaker-Zondag

Chiron and the Healing Journey: An Astrological and Psychological Perspective by Melanie Reinhart

Images of the Psyche: Exploring the Planets Through Psychology and Myth by Christine Valentine

The Inner Planets: Building Blocks of Personal Reality by Liz Greene and Howard Sasportas

The Magic Thread: Astrological Chart Interpretation Using Depth Psychology by Richard Idemon

Mythic Astrology by Ariel Guttman and Kenneth Johnson

Planetary Symbolism in the Horoscope by Karen Hamaker-Zondag

Saturn: A New Look at an Old Devil by Liz Greene

Aspects and Transits

The Gods of Change: Pain, Crisis and the Transits of Uranus, Neptune, and Pluto by Howard Sasportas

Planets in Aspect: Understanding Your Inner Dynamics by Robert Pelletier

Planets in Transit: Life Cycles for Living by Robert Hand

Saturn in Transit: Boundaries of Mind, Body, and Soul by Erin Sullivan

Chart Comparison

Planets in Composite: Analyzing Human Relationships by Robert Hand

Relationships and Life Cycles: Astrological Patterns of Personal Experience by Stephen Arroyo

Through the Looking Glass: A Search for the Self in the Mirror of Relationships by Richard Idemon

Miscellaneous

The Astrologer's Node Book by Donna Van Toen

Astrology for the Soul by Jan Spiller

Astrology and Spiritual Awakening by Gregory Bogart

Karmic Astrology: Joy and the Part of Fortune by Martin Schulman

Karmic Astrology: The Moon's Nodes and Reincarnation by Martin Schulman

Making the Gods Work for You: The Astrological Language of the Psyche by Caroline Casey

Prometheus the Awakener by Richard Tarnas

Your Secret Self: Illuminating the Mysteries of the Twelfth House by Tracy Marx

Also Consider Any Book by

Stephen Arroyo

Lynn Bell

Gregory Bogart

Darby Costello

Steven Forrest

Liz Greene

Robert Hand

Tracy Marx

Chani Nicholas

Howard Sasportas

Richard Tarnas

Astro Twins

Websites

https://mountainastrologer.com (online version of the magazine)

https://chaninicholas.com

https://www.jenniferfreed.com

https://astrostyle.com

https://www.astrograph.com

https://cafeastrology.com

https://astro.com

www.astroamerica.com (great astrology bookstore)

https://www.londonastrology.com (books and astrology supplies)

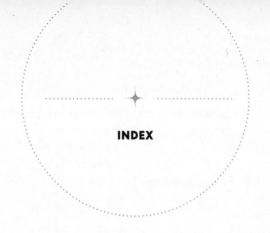

INDEX

ABOUT THE AUTHOR

Jennifer Freed, PhD, is a renowned psychological astrologer and social and emotional education trainer. She has spent over thirty-five years consulting with clients and businesses worldwide on psychological, spiritual, and educational topics. She has served as the clinical director of Pacifica Graduate Institute and a national consultant for EMDR (Post-Traumatic Growth Therapies). A regular contributor to goop and Maria Shriver's Sunday Paper, Jennifer has written ten books relating to personal growth. She has been interviewed by *The New York Times, The Wall Street Journal, USA Today, People,* and *Vogue.*